Welcom

[Handwritten note overlay:] To conference call.. / merge up to 5 calls / 1. Make a call / 2. Place call to another / 3. Tap Add Call / 4. Merge Call / Repeat to add chats

Nobody could hav... ...ugh to have bought
successful the iPho... ...have received one
be five years and six... ...considering buying
Launched in 2007 to... ...it in the future, then this
acclaim (it seems that only... ...u, as we walk you through
manufacturers were outwardly s... ...atures on every device, and the
about its chances) it's got slimmer, taller... latest version of Apple's mobile operating
and smarter with every release. system, iOS 6.

Now iPhone 5 is with us and it's the
most exciting iPhone ever. The retina
display is larger than it has been on any
previous iPhone, the camera is brighter,
the underlying processors are faster, and
there are more applications than ever
ready for download from the App Store.

No matter what its rivals do, they can't
generate the kind of excitement that
Apple does with every new iPhone, which
is all but guaranteed coverage not only in
the specialist media, but in newspapers
and magazines, on TV and radio news
programmes and online, right around
the world at the very point it's being
announced.

But don't turn away if you're still using
an iPhone 4 or 4S. These remain on sale
through the Apple Store and high street
phone chains, and they can both be
upgraded to iOS 6, too. They enjoy many
of the same features as the iPhone 5, and
so much of what we cover here is just as
relevant to these phones, too.

Over the pages that follow we'll show
you how to keep your iPhone secure, how
to browse the web and keep in touch with
friends by email, how to edit and share
your snaps in iPhoto and be productive
on the move in iWork, make sure you
never get lost, courtesy of Maps... and
much, much more.

Nik Rawlinson

Contents

154 GarageBand

108 Maps

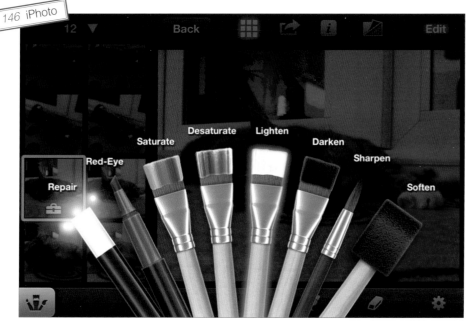

146 iPhoto

The Independent Guide to the
iPhone 5

WRITTEN BY Nik Rawlinson

ADVERTISING
MAGBOOK ACCOUNT MANAGER Katie Wood 07971 937162
SENIOR MAGBOOK EXECUTIVE Matt Wakefield 020 7907 6617
DIGITAL PRODUCTION MANAGER Nicky Baker 020 8907 6056

DENNIS PUBLISHING LTD
GROUP MANAGING DIRECTOR Ian Westwood
MANAGING DIRECTOR John Garewal
MD OF ADVERTISING Julian Lloyd-Evans
NEWSTRADE DIRECTOR David Barker
CHIEF OPERATING OFFICER Brett Reynolds
GROUP FINANCE DIRECTOR Ian Leggett
CHIEF EXECUTIVE James Tye
CHAIRMAN Felix Dennis

PUBLISHING AND MARKETING
MAGBOOK PUBLISHER Dharmesh Mistry 020 7907 6100
MARKETING EXECUTIVE Paul Goodhead 020 7907 6012

ZAGG®

25 YEAR PROTECTION

THE WORLD'S No. 1 SELLING SCREEN PROTECTION PRECISION CUT FOR YOUR APPLE iPhone®5. FIRST USED TO PROTECT U.S. MILITARY HELICOPTER BLADES FROM HIGH SPEED DAMAGE. THE invisibleSHIELD® IS THE PERFECT CHOICE FOR PROTECTING ANY DEVICE.

Available at:
ACCESSORYVILLAGE.co.uk

invisible® SHIELD

ORIGINAL

ZAGG® is dedicated to providing the most innovative and premium products for its customers.

WWW.ZAGG.COM

SCRATCH PROTECTION

MILITARY GRADE

NANO-MEMORY TECHNOLOGY™

25 YEAR GUARANTEE

PROTECT your iPhone®5

Section 1

Welcome to
the iPhone

Welcome to the iPhone

Who could ever have believed, at the time when Alexander Graham Bell invented the phone in 1876, that one day we would be walking around with so much power as this in our pockets?

The iPhone isn't simply a telephone. It's the perfect portable address book, a peerless hand-held browser, and the handiest mobile music player rolled into one. It's no wonder, then, that Apple kept it under such tight wraps in the years it took to develop, and that each new model is shrouded in secrecy right through its development cycle (notwithstanding the leaks and reveals that led up to the iPhone 5's unveiling).

Whatever iPhone you have, it will bear more than a passing similarity to the very first model. Under the hood, its operating system – iOS – will also share many common elements. iOS 6, the latest update, introduced a new maps

application, rationalised vouchers and tickets with Passbook, and syncs through iCloud. In this chapter we'll be taking a look at its most compelling features before exploring them in more depth in the chapters that follow.

Web browser

Before the iPhone, the web had been presented on phones and mobile devices in three ways: Wap, RSS or its native format. The latter of these three choices, native format, in which pages were shown as they were designed yet rendered on the smaller screen, was rarely successful. So, it must have been clear to Apple from the very first day its engineers sat down to plan the iPhone's development that if it was to include a web browser people would actually want to use, then it would have to make something more efficient, more impressive and far more usable than anything that had gone before it.

In short, it would have to display full-sized web pages on a tiny screen in their original format in such a way that it would seem they had been designed for just that format.

Apple achieved this in two ways. First, it gave the iPhone a truly massive resolution, so that even when shrunk down you would still be able to read headings and body text on most web pages. This resolution was enhanced with the arrival of the iPhone 4, which adopted

overview
mode of a
desktop computer
that fits the whole width
of a page in the window

retina
display
in which the
individual pixels were
too small to be detected by the
naked eye. In the iPhone 5 it's still 640
pixels wide, but now over 1000 pixels tall
thanks to the larger physical screen

Second, it let you tap to selectively
zoom in and out on the sections of a page
that you want to read in more detail. This
has been achieved in a more intelligent
way than you might imagine, as it's not
a dumb enlargement, but an accurate
zoom to mazimise the screen space given
to specific elements such as images or
columns of text.

The result was a browser that offered
the best of both worlds, taking the
tried and tested piecemeal peck and
pan approach of its predecessors and
supplementing it with the far superior

Email client

It's not so long ago that the only practical
way to keep up with your email on
the move was to buy a BlackBerry
Messenger. It took all of the responsibility
for managing your mail our of your hands,
delivering it as soon as it was received by
the server.

The iPhone does the same with
iCloud's @me.com addresses, and those
from a range of third-party providers.
What does this mean for you? Quite
simply, simplicity. Push takes all the
hassle out of mobile email, because the
messages come to you and can be dealt
with as soon and as often as you like. And
because the email is stored on Apple's
servers you can access it from any device
in any location. This means that any email

you mark as read on your Mac or PC will also be marked as read on your iPhone, and any email you send while you're out and about will also appear in the sent items folder on your computer.

As well as iCloud, the iPhone can connect to a host of other services including Yahoo mail, Gmail and regular Pop3 and IMAP services. For business users, it also works happily with Microsoft Exchange servers, which are common in enterprise set-ups.

It's important to choose the most appropriate server technology for your needs. While connecting to your own

Pop3 server is a simple way to use your regular email address on your iPhone, you won't be able to synchronise the read and unread status of your messages, or have a record of those messages sent from your iPhone on your regular computer, unless you cc the same messages back to yourself. IMAP does provide these features and for business users Exchange performs a similar function. Home users should consider hosting their domains on Google's App servers, which let them use the company's Gmail service under their own branding, thus benefiting from the IMAP features.

The iPhone mail client in its iPhone 4 and 4S (below) and iPhone 5 (right) incarnations showing relative sizes.

Maps

Online mapping is nothing new. We've had countless online street maps to choose from since the turn of the millennium. When the first iPhone appeared it used Google's map service for navigation, but with iOS 6 Apple switched this to its own variant.

This allows you to look up local businesses and services – such as car repair shops and pizza restaurants – and call them directly using the iPhone's telephony features. You can also set your iPhone to triangulate your position using

its built-in satellite navigation features (GPS on iPhone 4, GPS / GLANOS on iPhone 4S and iPhone 5).

This accepts incoming positional data from a satellite network to provide more precise information, plotting your location to within a metre or so. Like the network triangulation performed by the original iPhone, its accuracy does vary depending on a range of factors, such as cloud cover and your ability to see an open sky (so it won't work inside buildings unless you are next to a window), but the information it returns to the phone can be genuinely useful. Many applications now make use of it to provide location-based dating and games.

The old triangulation features haven't disappeared entirely, though. If the iPhone can't get a decent satellite fix it will use them as a fallback, and in all instances use this data to hone the satellite stream.

Camera

No phone worth its salts ships without a camera. How different that is to a decade ago when the networks were just starting to push the exciting idea of paying extortionate rates to send pictures to your friends. Now it's almost impossible to buy a new phone that doesn't have a camera, and even those of us who don't use them to send photos over the mobile network find them invaluable as digital notebooks when out shopping or spending time with family.

The first iPhone's camera was one of the biggest surprises when Steve Jobs revealed the gadget's final specifications.

Not because it was so advanced, like everything else inside its sleek glass and metal shell, but because in that first model it was comparably conservative. With a resolution of just two megapixels, the camera was easily outclassed by many cheaper competitors and looked like it was decided on well in advance of the iPhone actually going into production, at a time when such a pokey pixel count would have been the norm.

With the iPhone 5 we now have an eight-megapixel monster to play with, which you can focus by tapping on the screen and zoom digitally by spreading your fingers on the screen.

Photos are automatically geotagged by using the iPhone's built-in GPS receiver to mark them with the coordinates at which they were taken. These can then be used for filing, or for presenting your images on a map. They are also understood by services like sharing site Flickr.

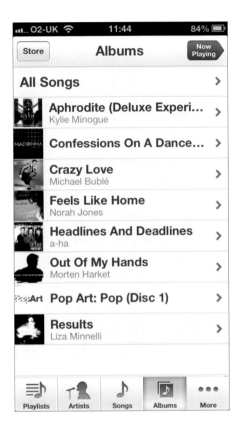

Contacts

The iPhone blows even the best mobile address book out of the water, with a fully fledged contact management system that can handle names, numbers, addresses and even photos. It synchronises with your Mac or PC, so that the numbers on your phone match the ones on your computer and on iCloud.

Extra fields let you tap on an email address to start writing a message, tap an address to see it plotted on a map and tap a URL to open it in Safari. Everything is tracked by Spotlight making it quick and easy to find friends and family.

Music and movie player

The iPhone features three key media apps. First, **iTunes**, which allows you to download music and videos from the iTunes Store. This media is organised by type in either **Music** (above) or **Videos**. These do just what you'd expect, playing back your purchases and any media you have transferred from your Mac or PC. The Music application understands the concept of playlists, allowing you to organise your music according to circumstance or play a shuffled selection.

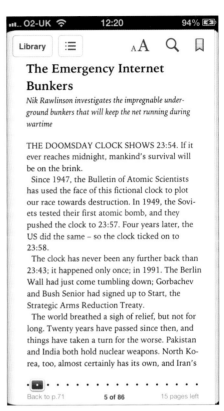

iBooks turns your iPhone into a pocket ebook reader, complete with full-colour covers, clearly-rendered text and a built-in book store selling the latest blockbusters.

The videos application plays your media full-screen in landscape orientation, giving you the best possible portable environment in which to catch on on movies that you don't have time to watch at home.

Each of these applications is compatible with Apple's AirPlay system, allowing you to play back your media on a regular television or external speakers using AirPlay hardware, such as Apple TV or AirPort Express. These represent separate purchases, but thanks to their seamless integration greatly enhance the iPhone experience.

iBooks

Apple is hoping to do the same for ebooks as it has for music, selling digital products through its own online store.

Buying is quick and easy, as the store uses the same login credentials as the iTunes Store and iCloud.

Mainstream books are generally slightly cheaper than the equivalent printed volumes, and many out-of-copyright books, such as Pride and Prejudice or Emma, are free.

Because iBooks uses the industry standard ePub format you can download a lot of other books that don't appear in Apple's own store from online book repositories such as Project Gutenberg, and upload them to your iPhone through the Document Sharing pane in iTunes.

Newsstand

As well as digital books, many iPhone owners use their handsets to read magazines to which they subscribe. Although there are dedicated publishing channels, such as the Zinio news stand, many publishers prefer to publish magazines on the App Store.

Newsstand (below left) simplifies the task of keeping your subscriptions under control and up to date, by providing one central app through which you can organise your incoming magazines, with a direct link to the store to buy new issues.

Passbook

Passbook (below) performs a similar function to Newsstand in unifying a wide range of third-party applications into one single app. It lets you keep all of your loyalty cards, vouchers and tickets in one place so that you don't have to have them scattered around your various home screens.

Social networking

Twitter and Facebook are both built in to iOS 6. Twitter had been a part of the iPhone since iOS 5, but Facebook integration was likely sooner or later.

By building in these social networks at the very core of its mobile operating

system, Apple makes it easy to share content, including photos, with your contacts, as Facebook and Twitter appear on the sharing shortcuts built into its pre-installed applications.

The iOS Twitter and Facebook features work hand in hand with the Twitter (below) and Facebook apps, which are free downloads from the App Store.

Reminders

Reminders (below right) is a fairly simple tool in which to track a list of jobs that need to be completed. You don't have to tap them out in order, so can pop them in whenever they occur to you. You can then set reminders based on either an arbitrary deadline or a location.

So, if you have to make a phone call at 3pm, you'd enter that with a deadline of 15:00 hrs. Alternatively, if you knew that you needed to buy apples the next time you're passing by the grocer's shop, but

didn't know when that would be, you'd set a reminder based on location. Your iPhone would then use its built-in GPS receiver to track your location, and when it detected that you were near the grocer's it would pop up a reminder that you should go in and buy your apples.

Reminders appear on screen in the middle of the display, accompanied by an audible beep (assuming you haven't muted the speaker) and a short vibration.

iMessage

Apple has rewritten the iPhone's default SMS application – Messages – to add a new feature called iMessage. This also works on the iPod touch and iPad, allowing you to send an unlimited number of free messages to other iOS users who have upgraded to version 5 or 6.

Each message is threaded with those that come before and after it to present an easy-to-follow conversation stream,

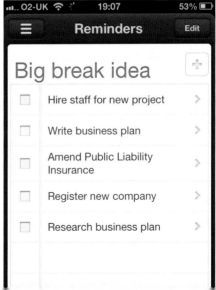

and individual postings even appear in bubbles (see grab, right).

By synchronising across each device, you can leave off a conversation on your iPhone and continue later when using your iPad or Mac, if you have one.

Wifi networking

The iPhone is no dumb telephone – it has a variety of communications tools built in, with Bluetooth (see below) and wireless, or 'wifi', networking supplementing its range of mobile features. Wifi is the same networking protocol as that used by wireless computers, laptops, home routers and modems. It is also commonly found in workplaces and coffee shops, enabling iPhone owners to browse the web without paying high fees to the mobile networks. In the iPhone 5 it has been upgraded to 5GHz.

Bluetooth

The iPhone's third means of wireless connectivity is Bluetooth. This is slower than wireless networking and has a shorter range, with most devices incapable of transmitting further than about 10 metres. So while technically feasible, this radio technology would never be a truly practical means of efficiently transferring large blocks of data or surfing the web. For most iPhone owners, its use will, therefore, largely be confined to transferring photos and other small chunks of data, or connecting to a wireless Bluetooth headset.

So why still use such a short-range, slow technology? Simply that it has one major benefit: widespread compatibility. Bluetooth devices are able to see each other when in range and, because they have built-in 'profiles' that describe their features and abilities, they are able to inform each other of how they can interact. This allows for easy set-up, with little or no input from users, making Bluetooth the ideal communications technology for those of us who want things to 'just work'. It also allows you to connect a Bluetooth keyboard so that you can more practically use office

2.5G chips used in the original iPhone) with a GPS receiver. It did it, though, and has now supplemented it with GLANOS satellite reception.

With GPS features built-in, you will always know exactly where you are at any time and, as a bonus, can use your iPhone to plan routes.

By combining information data with maps drawn down from Apple's servers, the Maps application can plot the fastest route between your current location and any other spot (or, indeed, between two locations even if you aren't currently standing at your origin or destination). It can take traffic into account, and gives you the option of providing route details for driving, public transport or walking, with journey length and expected journey times detailed.

On-screen keyboard

The iPhone has done away with physical buttons. Apart from the power button, ringer switch, volume control and Home button, there are no external moving parts on the iPhone, as all of the other buttons have been moved into the software realm and are rendered as graphics on the touchscreen – including the regular keyboard (see above, left).

This is very intelligent, and while the keys are small (how else would you fit them all onto the screen in portrait mode?), the iPhone's touch-sensitive membrane is accurate enough to sense where your fingers are falling and magnify each button as you press it, greatly increasing most users' accuracy.

applications such as Pages, Numbers and Keynote, without having to spend all of your time tapping away on the small on-screen equivalent.

Satellite navigation

Having been absent from the first model, GPS features were long-rumoured for inclusion in an upgrade, but until the 3G arrived, nobody could be quite sure whether Apple's engineers would have been able to integrate an upgraded communications chip (3G hardware draws more power than the

Don't believe us? Well, think back to the first time you started to use T9 predictive messaging. If you were anything like us, you probably spent a lot of time looking at the screen and trying to work out how you could create each word as you typed, so great was the required mind-shift in the move from picking out characters individually. Soon, though, you learned not to think about how it worked, but to just get on with things and – you know what – by the power of technology it did what you wanted, and eight times out of 10, it got the word you wanted.

Treat your iPhone's on-screen keyboard in a similar way and you will not go far wrong. As an added bonus, because the iPhone does not have a hard-wired keyboard like a BlackBerry or a traditional non-stylus PDA, it means that Apple can quickly integrate new features, such as a wider range of languages in updated editions.

Even if you have set your language to English, you can still access a wide variety of international characters using the regular iPhone keyboard simply by holding down your finger on the character closest to the one you want. Hold for long enough and up will pop a menu of alternate, related, accented international characters for you to choose from.

Home screen

The Home screen is where you'll find the icons and buttons that link you to every other application on your iPhone. It includes a range of information elements, such as network coverage and strength, wifi availability and remaining battery power as well as the current time. You can return to the Home screen at any time by pressing the circular button on the bottom of the iPhone's front surface. You can also rearrange the application icons by holding down on an icon until they all start to shiver. At this point they can be dragged into their new positions.

By dragging one icon on top of another you can group them together into a folder. This is indicated by a black box with a white rounded border that expands when you tap on it. The first time you create a folder you can change its name from the one your iPhone suggests. You can then drag other apps onto the folder icon to add them.

Phone

With so many other features, the iPhone's actual phone component becomes something of an 'also-ran' tool, as it is almost crowded out by more exciting offerings such as the music player, web browser, mapping applications and the fully automated email client.

Yet there it is, sitting square and centre, and well integrated with a whole raft of other tools, including Contacts and Maps from which it can draw supplementary data. It features call holding and conference calling, which while they are also found on other mobile phones, is better built and easier to use on the iPhone than on most of its rivals. In the next section we'll take a closer look at the iPhone's key features, and how you can put them to best use.

The Stunning iPhone 5 Collection

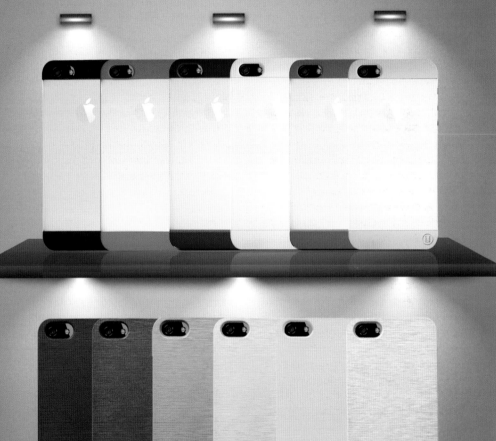

A*GIS*

iPhone 5

The iPhone 5 took a long time to appear. Most Apple watchers had been expecting the company to follow up its phenomenally successful iPhone 4 with the iPhone 5 a year earlier but, as we now know, that didn't happen. Instead the company once again took the tried-and-trusted road that it trod when upgrading the iPhone 3G, producing a new model in essentially the same case with an upgraded camera and faster processor. This didn't warrant a completely new version number, so as with the move from 3G to 3GS, the company simply added an 'S' to give us the all new iPhone 4S.

Finally, though, on 12 September 2012, Apple CEO Tim Cook took to the stage at an event that was covered in mainstream press worldwide to announce iPhone 5.

It went on sale a week later, with Apple retaining the iPhone 4 and 4S in its line-up to cater for less demanding users, buyers on a budget and those who want a free phone with a contract.

Under the hood

So what would we find if we pulled an iPhone 5 to pieces?

At its heart is the A6 processor, Apple's most advanced mobile processor to date. Apple claims that this delivers up to twice the processing power and graphics speed of the A5 found in the iPhone 4S, which itself was twice as fast as the A4 in the iPhone 4, with seven times

faster grahics. Over the last couple of generations, then, the iPhone's underlying hardware has been significantly upgraded, which is great news for games players. The iPod touch, which was updated at the same time and traditionally mimicks the iPhone's specs pretty closely, has a slower processor under the hood, so although it looks similar and also runs iOS 6, it's unlikely to perform quite so snappily.

Super smart snapper

The rear camera was one area in which Apple chose to leave things as they were, physically, retaining the 8 megapixel resolution of the iPhone 4S. This has 60% more pixels than featured on the camera in the iPhone 4, and four times the number found in the original iPhone's rather disappointing two megapixel device.

iPhone 5 also uses the same f/2.4 aperture arrangement as the iPhone 4S, which again was an improvement on that offered in the iPhone 4, whose aperture was a slightly dimmer f/2.8. However, in the iPhone 5 it has changed the glass used in the lens in front of the sensor to saphire crystal, which is not only clearer but also more durable.

The iPhone 4S and 5's bright, wide aperture has a side benefit over the narrower aperture in the iPhone 4: it allows the camera to focus more

accurately on a smaller area, so if you use the iPhone 4S or 5 to take portrait shots of your friends and family you'll find that it's easier to pull them forward from the blackground, which will become naturally blurred.

So, although the headline resolution hasn't changed, the rear camera is nonetheless improved in many ways, and that's before you get to the improvements in its underlying software, which now lets you shoot panorama images of up to 28

megapixels, automatically stitched and colour-corrected, simply by sweeping your phone in an arc across the scene in front of you.

Of course, eight megapixels is a lot of data to process and save in a very short space of time – especially if you want your users to be able to take another photo almost right away, which brings us back to the A6 processor, into which Apple has built a dedicated image signal processor to hurry things along. The result

should be a more responsive experience all round.

At the front of the case there's long been a second camera, and while there was no change to this component in the move from iPhone 4 to iPhone 4S, the iPhone 5 sees a significant improvement, as it now supports a resolution of 1.2 megapixeld – up from 0.3 megapixels VGA – and 720p video recording. It is now also built with the components behind the sensors rather than in front (so-called Back Side Illumination) which allows it to gather more light for a brighter, better-exposed result.

Movie-making magic

The camera isn't only suited to shooting stills, though. Since the arrival of the 3GS it has had movie-making skills, saving high quality video to the camera roll.

Apple accompanied the introduction of the iPhone 4S with the porting of iMovie from the Mac to iOS to take advantage of its heightened video recording prowess. The video features of the iPhone 5 remain the same with full HD recording at 1080p (1920 x 1080 pixels, progressive), which is ripe for playing back on a regular computer or TV, either by burning it to DVD or using iOS's built-in AirPlay hooks to send it to an Apple TV device or other Apple computer running OS X 10.8 Mountain Lion.

The iPhone 5 may be small, but it's accomplisted, and with image stabilisation features you should be able to take your iPhone to more locations and still capture very acceptable footage.

Siri (above) integrates with many of iOS's core features, such as the Reminders app, to offer an alternative to the virtual keyboard. Despite being software-based, it doesn't work on iPhone 4 or earlier.

Design

The iPhone 4S's physical design was perhaps the biggest disappointment at the launch event, simply because it didn't change as much as everyone had been led to believe it would.

Prior to its unveiling there had been rumours and mock-ups of a slimmer, trimmer device with a thinner body and a gently sloping back. That turned out to be inaccurate – just like the rumours and speculation surrounding a larger screen.

From the outside Apple produced essentially a rerun of its previous entrant into the smartphone market, with the same glass front and back, held together by a band of antennae running around the edge. For anyone upgrading from the iPhone 4, of course, this was good news as it meant they could take all of their add-ons and accessories, such as cases and hands-free in-car cradles with them and use them on the iPhone 4S.

However, much of what we had been expecting in the new device did appear when the iPhone 5 finally shipped, including the thinner case. Apple claims that the iPhone 5 is the slimmest smartphone available, and it's now taller than it was in its previous incarnation, with a 4in screen playing host to five rows of application icons.

The only physical buttons on the whole device are dotted around the edge, covering off power, volume and muts. There's one button on the front of the case, as usual. This is the large circular home button . Whatever you happen to be doing on your phone at any time, pressing this sends that app into the background and returns you to the home screen. Holding down this button and briefly pressing the power button on the top of the case saves whatever is on the screen at the time as an image file in your Camera Roll.

Network features

The iPhone 5's connectivity features were inproved for use on both your own wifi network and the cellphone network.

For starters it now supports 5GHz wifi, which should be more responsive on a compatible local network as it should suffer from less interference from competing products on the same network.

On the cell network front, it is Apple's first phone to support so-called 4G. These networks are still being rolled out in many countries, and even in those where they have been introduced, coverage is not often nationwide, so it is able to fall back on earlier standards, as used by the iPhone 4 and iPhone 4S. Indeed, it remains compatible with the Edge network technology that hosted the very first iPhone six model generations ago.

The iPhone 4S and 5 support both CDMA and GSM connections in a single unit, and the iPhone 5 supports the 1800MHz version of 4G, but not any of the other versions, so bear this in mind when choosing your carrier.

Siri: your personal assistant

The most radical addition to the iPhone 4S was Siri, a voice-enabled personal assistant that largely does away with the need to use the keyboard to perform common tasks. It's available on iPhone 5, and some features appear on the updated iPod touch running iOS 6.

Apple acquired the technology that underpins Siri and then set about building

an enormous data centres that, although linked to iCloud, could also help to deliver responses to Siri users' spoken queries.

In Apple's own words, Siri is 'an intelligent assistant that helps you get things done just by asking. Siri understands context allowing you to speak naturally when you ask it questions, for example, if you ask "Will I need an umbrella this weekend?" it understands you are looking for a weather forecast. Siri is also smart about using the personal information you allow it to access, for example, if you tell Siri "Remind me to call Mom when I get home" it can find "Mom" in your address book, or ask Siri "What's the traffic like around here?" and it can figure out where "here" is based on your current location. Siri helps you make calls, send text messages or email, schedule meetings and reminders, make notes, search the Internet, find local businesses, get directions and more. You can also get answers, find facts and even perform complex calculations just by asking.'

Google has been working on similar voice recognition features, designed for use on rival phones running its Android operating system.

Siri hooks in to many of the core iOS applications, such as Maps, Messages and Reminders, providing a full replacement for the keyboard and even extending dictation features to apps such as Mail, courtesy of a Siri microphone icon on the software keyboard.

Siri's responses to most requests will be context sensitive, either dealing

Choosing an iPhone for you

Although the iPhone 5 jumps straight in at the top of Apple's product line-up, and the company resisted the temptation to introduce a feature-poor, cheaper model lower down in its product heirarchy, the old iPhone 4 and iPhone 4S models remain on sale for cash-strapped users who don't need all of the new features offered by the latest version.

Being lower-priced they will also enable network operators to offer them as free inducements to sign up to an ongoing contract.

Use this table to see what you'll be missing if you choose not to upgrade to the latest, greatest model, and whether you could make a saving by opting for something a little cheaper.

When choosing an iPhone, be sure to factor in the cost of the ongoing contract, without which you'll miss out on many of the most compelling features and bear in mind that over the length of its duration it can cost you far more than the up-front price of the phone. Paying a little more for the handset in exchange for a cheaper monthly bill can therefore pay dividends.

iPhone 5

Capacities
64GB, 32GB, 16GB

Camera features
8 megapixels
Face detection
f/2.4 aperture
Front 1.2mp camera
Flash

Video features
1080p resolution
30 frames per second
Video stabilisation
LED light

Screen
1136 x 640 pixels

Battery life
8 hours 3G talk
10 hours wifi browsing
225 hours standby

Wireless features
802.11b/g/n/wifi
Bluetooth 4

Weight
112g

Dimensions (HxWxD)
123.8 x 58.6 x 7.6mm

Available colours
Black and slate / white and silver

with replies to incoming messages or providing answers to spoken web requests with reference to the iPhone's current location, which can be derived from the GPS chip, through triangulation of cellphone masts or the IP address of your wifi Internet connection. So, ask what the weather will be like this afternoon and Siri will be able to tell you, after pulling down the answer from one of a range of online data sources, including search engines Bing, Google and Yahoo, and directories like Yell.

The only potential downside is that Siri requires an Internet connection so that it can pass the contents of your query to Apple's servers, so needs wifi, 3G or 4G coverage.

iPhone 4S

Capacities
16GB

Camera features
8 megapixels
Face detection
f/2.4 aperture
Front VGA camera
Flash

Video features
1080p resolution
30 frames per second
Video stabilisation
LED light

Screen
960 x 640 pixels

Battery life
7 hours 3G talk
9 hours wifi browsing
200 hours standby

Wireless features
802.11b/g/n/wifi
Bluetooth 4

Weight
140g

Dimensions (HxWxD)
115.2 x 58.6 x 9.3mm

Available colours
Black / white

iPhone 4

Capacities
8GB

Camera features
5 megapixels
Front VGA camera
Flash

Video features
720p resolution
30 frames per second
LED light

Screen
960 x 640 pixels

Battery life
7 hours 3G talk
10 hours wifi browsing
300 hours standby

Wireless features
802.11b/g/n/wifi
Bluetooth 2.1+EDR

Weight
137g

Dimensions (HxWxD)
115.2 x 58.6 x 9.3mm

Available colours
Black / white

Siri

Siri is Apple's personal assistant. It first appeared on iPhone 4S, but with the introduction of iOS 6 it is now also found on the iPhone 5, 'new' (Third Generation) iPad and, to a slightly limited degree, the iPod touch announced in Septeber 2012 alongside the iPhone 5.

Siri conception

Apple didn't actually invent Siri. It was initially developed by Siri Inc – hence the name – and sold through the iOS App Store. Apple saw the genius in the application, and how useful it could be in advancing the iPhone's hands-free features, and snapped up the company and development team. It took Siri development in house, cancelled any existing plans to port the technology to competing BlackBerry and Android platforms and eventually took the service offline entirely in the run up to the launch of the iPhone 4S.

At the same time it was building an impressive data centre in Maiden, North Carolina, that would form the backbone of its online services, including iCloud and Siri, and when the iPhone 4S launched in late 2011 it was with Siri firmly in place, providing web services and impressively accurate dictation tools.

However, it wasn't perfect. It only supported four languages at launch – English, German, French and Japanese – and performance outside of the United Stated was variable as it hadn't been fully localised to know about national traffic systems and businesses.

Siri today

That second factor is still true to a degree. Siri's performance is still better inside the United States than anywhere else in the world, although Apple is adding new features to the coverage it gives for international users.

Further, it has expanded the range of languages that Siri can understand and in which it can provide answers to nine, and now caters for the Italian and Chinese markets. The latter is particularly important as Apple looks to become a dominant mobile force in that country.

Using Siri doesn't require any knowledge of how to use a database – you simple hold down the Home button and then speak your request.

How do I use Siri?

Siri doesn't assume any technical expertise. You don't even need to type anything to use it; it's all controlled by your voice. Neither do you need to learn any arcane instructions or commands: you just talk to it in plain English.

If you've seen Star Trek you'll know how the crew of the Enterprise talk to their onboard computer in plain English. Siri works in a similar fashion.

You start by holding down the Home button until the Siri icon appears at the bottom of the screen (see opposite page). It looks like a silver button with a microphone in the middle. Tap this and speak your command, such as 'what will the weather be like tomorrow', or 'remind me to phone home on Friday morning'.

Siri will pass your command back to Apple's data centre where the remote voice recognition applications will analyse the sound wave and pull out recognised words and phrases. These will be further analysed to discern their meaning and then used as the basis of your query. If it was a request for information it will do its best to answer it with reference to the web and online databases. If it was an instruction or a command that can be performed by your iPhone, it is passed back to the device and the relevant local application takes over from there.

Unlike early Mac- and PC-based voice recognition tools, you don't need to give

Siri can answer questions, or let you interact directly with other iOS applications without using the keyboard.

Siri any training before you start using it, as it is being trained and improved all the time because it's being used by so many people around the world simultaneously.

When it first launched it had some trouble with some regional accents including, famously, some Scottish voices, but Apple claims that as more people interact with Siri and it learns how to interpret what they say this should become less of an issue.

What can Siri tell me?

Siri works by hooking into a range of online databases, but the information that it pulls out of them and its relevance to your queries depends very much on the country from which you're accessing them. In general, though, Siri has a good general knowledge and can tailor the information that it passes back to be relevant to your local area.

For example, you could ask 'will it be cold tomorrow?' and Siri will check the local forecast. Because your iPhone has an integrated GPS receiver it already knows where you are located, so doesn't need you to specify '...in Edinburgh' or '...in Paris' to give you the correct information. However, tacking that kind of location onto the end of your request will allow you to look up information relevant to places where you aren't currently standing. More generalised requests could simply be globally-relevant answers, such as 'how many grams are there in a pound'.

Some information is patchy or simply unavailable outside of the United States at the time of writing. For example, traffic conditions work well inside the US but aren't available in the United Kingdom. Likewise, when iOS 6 was announced Apple simultaneously annouced that Siri would be able to provide American Football sports results, but didn't announce an equivalent feature for UK-based football teams playing what US users would call 'soccer'. Over time this is likely to change as Siri's repertoire improves.

Siri is a mine of information, and can return accurate answers to a wide range of topical questions, and offers to search the web if it can't answer itself.

Siri with other iOS applications

Some Siri requests don't require that the servers pass back the answer to a question, but that they instruct a core iOS application to perform a function.

For example, you can text people directly by saying 'text Alan I am running five minutes late', or you could set an appointment in your diary by telling Siri 'remind me that it's Alan's birthday on Monday'. Because you had specified no time, Siri would enter this as a whole-day event.

Thanks to your iPhone's built-in GPS receiver, Siri knows where you're asking questions from, so can provide geographically accurate results.

Siri's personality

Siri is very personable and has his or her own personality (Siri's gender varies from country to country, depending on who is providing the voice). This allows him or her to carry on a conversation with you, where one question can draw on the results of the previous request. So, you could ask 'Who is the president of France?' and when Siri gives you an answer it would understand that a following question along the lines of 'how old is he' still relates to the French leader.

Siri understands

When it launched as part or the iPhone 4S, Siri understood only English, French, German and Japanese, but with the introduction of enhanced features in iOS 6 that number has now been increased to nine languages, covering:

- English
- French
- German
- Japanese
- Spanish
- Italian
- Korean
- Mandarin
- Cantonese

iPhone 4 users

Siri was incorporated into iPhone 4S as an incentive for iPhone 4 users to upgrade their handsets as otherwise there would be little to differentiate the two. Although it has been retrospectively rolled out to the 'new' iPad it won't be retrospectively made available to iPhone 4.

Users of that phone therefore have only limited voice control tools at their disposal, with voice dialling, which allows you to call a contact in your address book without typing their number in the phone application.

If they aren't stored in your Contacts list you won't even be able to do this. However, voice dialling remains useful for hands-free calling from cars.

Find My iPhone and Lost Mode

Apple recognises that as we take our iPhone everywhere we go, there is always a chance we could lose it.

This might be completely innocent, as we could leave it on the bus or in the back of a taxi, or it could be more malicious with our gadgets stolen from our pockets or bags.

However you happen to be parted from your iPhone, though, you want the best chance possible of finding it again or, if it's been taken dishonestly, at least of removing all of your data to keep it safe from prying eyes.

That's where Find My iPhone comes in. Originally developed to calm business users' worries about data loss it's a boon for consumers, too. The name is slightly misleading, though, as its functions and abilities have grown enormously over the years, and it can now also be used to track a missing iPad, iPod touch, and even regular Apple computers.

What is Find My iPhone

Find my iPhone is a smart service that uses Apple's iCloud to locate your iPhone anywhere in the world.

It relies on you having at least one iCloud email account active on the handset and it being set to receive push email. If you don't get have this set up, tap Settings | Mail, Contacts, Calendars | Add Account... and select iCloud from the list of account type options. If you do already ave an iCloud account active on your device, ensure it is set up to use push email.

Activate Find My iPhone

Find my iPhone is turned off by default. This makes sense as it relies on passing your current location through the iCloud servers, which some users may consider to be a security risk. To turn it on, tap Settings | iCloud and tap the ON/OFF slider. Although it's now active you needn't worry that your iPhone is sending

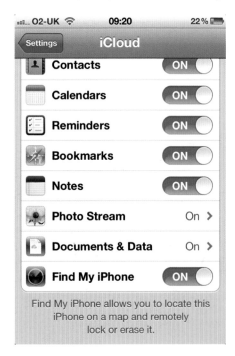

Find My iPhone allows you to locate this iPhone on a map and remotely lock or erase it.

its location out to all and sundry; it'll only disclose its position when specifically requested through the iCloud website, which is where we're heading next.

Now log in to your account at *icloud. com/#find*.

Right away iCloud starts searching for each of the devices that you have registered to your account and plotting them on a map. You can switch between them by clicking each one in the Devices panel, and switch between zoomable map, satellite and hybrid views to help you zoom in to the closest possible location.

Select the device that you need to locate and it will be highlighted on the

map using a small green pushpin. You can zoom in for a better look.

At the same time, a floating panel appears in the top right of the window giving you three options: play sound, lost mode and erase iPhone. You should work through each option in turn.

Play sound simply makes the iPhone beep and display a button on screen to cancel it. This will help you find your iPhone if you've lost it in your home or somewhere close by, and will work even if the iPhone it set to mute.

If that doesn't help you find your phone, the likelihood is that it's further away than you expected. That's when you should step up to Lost Mode.

Find my iPhone plots the position of your iPhone on a regular Google Map or satellite view, along with any iPads, iPod touches and Apple computers you own.

Lost Mode

Lost Mode locks your phone by applying your regular passcode and displays a message on screen asking whoever has it in their posession to call you so you can arrange for its return. You should always use it with care and make sure that you don't give away any personal information that could be used to track you or argree to meet anywhere but a public place.

Lost Mode will lock the phone and put an alert on the screen asking whoever has it to call you, which they can do by tapping the green Call button (see right) without having access to the rest of the phone's functions.

The whole time your iPhone is in Lost Mode, it will keep on sending back updates about its location whenever you check in through iCloud, with emails arriving in your inbox containing a map of its position. This will help law enforcement officials to find the current posessor of a stolen phone if you pass the details on.

Erase iPhone

The erase option should be your final recourse. As its name suggests, it deletes all of the data from your phone but, at the same time, will stop you from tracking its position any more.

Only perform this action if you are therefore certain that you aren't going to get the phone back, and so the most important thing to preserve is your privacy, rather than your hardware and digital content.

iGlaze for iPhone

minimalist protection for your iPhone 5

Perfectly slim fit
with iPhone 5.

Designed and tested to
be "flash-friendly".

All buttons and ports
are easily accessible.

Calculator   Calendar   Camer

Music   Maps   Messag

Notes   Phone   Photo

280

23°

iOS 6

What is iOS 6?

iOS – previously known as iPhone OS – is Apple's operating system for the iPhone, iPad, iPod touch and Apple TV. It doesn't run the same applications as OS X on the Mac but is built on the same codebase.

The manifestation that appears on these devices is only one half of the equation, with the second half being the software development kit (SDK) that Apple makes available to paying developers so that they can write applications for the devices that run it. To this end, iOS is now one of the best supported operating systems on any platform – not just on smartphones – with over half a million applications produced to date. These can be downloaded directly from the iOS App Store application on the iPhone, or through iTunes on a regular Mac or PC.

iOS also hooks in to iCloud, Apple's online backup and synchronisation service, which copies iWorks documents between your mobile device and a Mac, and automatically transfers photos taken on your iPhone to either iPhoto or Aperture on the Mac, or a dedicated folder on a PC, at the same time syncing apps and media downloads.

It has a built-in Software Update tool that makes it easy to check that you're running the most up-to-date version of the operating system, and a built-in app store that lets you buy new applications directly without reverting to your Mac or PC. This separately keeps track of any updates

to your purchases over time and lets you download free upgrades.

The Notification Center, which was introduced in iOS 5, centralises all of the messages and alerts spawned by your applications into one easy to find location so you don't have to cancel them all individually. Swipe down from the clock above any app to open it.

Complex underneath, but so simple on top. iOS is a carefully crafted operating system designed to be easily controlled by a tap or swipe of the finger.

iOS 6

iOS 6, as its name suggests, is the sixth iteration of the operating system. It was finally made available to the general public in late summer 2012 after several months of testing among the developer community. It is a free update for users of later iPhones and iPads, but as with its

iOS 6's Software Update feature compares the version of the operating system you are running with the most recent version on Apple's servers.

predecessors it won't work on the earliest iPhone models, some early iPod touches, or the iPhone 3G as they don't have the necessary hardware to support it. Such obsolescence is also a good way for Apple to encourage us to upgrade.

How does it differ from iOS 5?

If you were just to look at the home screen of an iPhone running iOS 6 you could be forgiven for thinking that nothing had changed in the move from iOS 5. All of the familiar icons and folders remain in place, Spotlight stays where it always was and your most commonly-used applications can still be organied on a short Dock that appears on each of the Home Screens.

This is misleading, though, as beneath the surface there are many fundamental changes that make the operating system both more robust and more flexible.

iOS 6 introduces a number of brand new applications, including Passbook, which works in much the same way as the Newsstand app that first appeared in iOS 5. Where Newsstand provided a single unified folder to contain digital magazine and newspaper downloads, Passbook does the same for loyalty cards, tickets, membership cards and vouchers. This should mean that you can do away with many of the bespoke loyalty applications you have downloaded from coffee shops and other retailers, and free up space on your home screens.

The Maps application has also had a serious overhaul. Its content was previously provided by Google, but map data is now supplied directly from Apple's own servers, while directions come from the navigation experts at Tom Tom. It has a fresh new look as a result, and maintains the ability to display satellite photography.

This move away from reliance on Google has also seen Apple drop the YouTube application. This had been a resident of the iPhone and iPod touch since their very earliest days, and they provided the best means of viewing YouTube videos on any Apple device. Going forward from the introduction of iOS 6, though, we'll have to watch YouTube videos through the Safari browser or use a third-party client.

Facebook is now integrated, just like Twitter, and Siri, Apple's voice-recognition assistant, has been upgraded across several territories so that it now knows more about cinema times, sports venues and so on.

Mixed in are myriad tiny improvements just waiting to be discovered...

Notification Center keeps all of your messages in one place, doing away with the multiple pop-ups of earlier releases.

Passbook is new to iOS 6. It introduces a unified folder for all of your loyalty cards, tickets and voucher applications.

XtremeMac

Tango™ Air

AirPlay® Technology Wireless Hi-Fi Speaker

Features two tweeters, two mid-range and one active subwoofer for staggering sound quality in a flexible design that maintains its audio integrity whether the speaker is positioned vertically or horizontally. With built-in AirPlay technology and simple plug & pull setup through iOS 5.0 or greater, you'll enjoy access to your entire music library through your wireless network.

Also available: XtremeMac™ Sportwraps

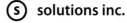

Key concepts

Where have all my buttons gone?

The most immediate difference between the iPhone and a regular mobile is the lack of a keypad. This is both a blessing and a curse, the latter being that there is no tactile feedback for sight-impaired users. This also means you can easily slip and press more than one virtual button at once, although the iPhone has always been fairly talented when it comes to guessing what you meant and, in a forgiving manner, tends to use the key you meant, even if you pressed one of those that surrounds it.

However, for the vast majority of users, and those less egotistic than the serial self-portrait takers, it is an excellent implementation, and a few minutes spent getting used to the way it works will repay very real and long-term dividends.

The first thing to realise is that the keyboard is intelligent in two very subtle ways. First, it briefly enlarges each key as you tap it, so you can see its key cap pop up above your finger to make sure you have pressed the right one (and almost every time you will, because it is clever enough to sense the most likely key you were aiming for). Second, it offers to auto-complete words for you by dropping a suggested completion for partially entered words immediately below the cursor. The built-in default dictionary adapts to your needs quickly, and after entering a unique word just once or twice

– your surname, for example – it will be offering to complete that for you, too. To accept its suggestion, just press whatever key would come immediately after the word – a space, the enter key and so on.

Finger gestures

You can frequently do away with the keyboard altogether, because the iPhone uses your fingers in much the same way as a regular computer uses a mouse. On-screen buttons can be tapped to navigate through menus, while double-tapping some elements, such as columns on a web page, will expand them to fill the screen, without you even defining the edges of the text.

Other elements can be swiped, such as album covers in the iPod and pictures in the photos application, which can be slid onto and off the screen just like real-life picture prints on a table.

The cleverest of all the finger gestures, though, is the pinch and reverse-pinch (right), which will zoom in and out on various on-screen elements. Test this out by starting Maps, typing in your postcode and then putting your thumb and forefinger in the centre of the screen, both pressed together. Slowly open them up and see how the map expands with them as you zoom in. Doing the same in reverse will zoom out again. This same trick works in several other applications, including photos and websites.

Pinch or stretch your fingers to zoom in and out on the iPhone's display.

Magnified selections

The iPhone screen may be high resolution, and it is certainly much larger than those found on older mobile phones, but it is still a fairly limited space in which to fit a whole touch-sensitive operating system, with input boxes, graphics and a keyboard. Apple's software engineers have, fortunately, acknowledged this and integrated a magnifier (next page), which pops up automatically whenever the iPhone judges it may be required.

Test it by firing up the web browser (the Safari icon on the bar at the bottom

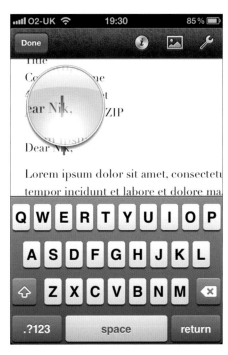

of the Home screen), entering a web address and, once the page has loaded, holding down your finger over that address on the input bar. A magnifier will pop up and follow your finger as you move to the left and right through the text.

The swivelling screen

Even in its portrait orientation, the iPhone's screen resolution is so high that it is fairly easy to read the text on many regular, plain websites, such as the BBC News site. However, several applications also work in landscape mode, literally spinning around on the screen as you turn the iPhone on its side, thanks to the integrated orientation sensor.

Calculator is one of many applications whose mode depends on orientation, offering more features in landscape.

Not all applications are appropriate to landscape use, but those that are really benefit. Moreover, it makes web pages much more readable by giving on-screen text room to breathe.

Some applications only work in one mode or the other while others change their mode altogether, the most notable example being iPod, which displays menus in portrait mode, and album art when tipped on one side, and the Calculator displays a regular adding machine in portrait mode, and a scientific calculator when turned on its side.

Copy and paste arrived in the third iteration of Apple's iPhone software, and plugged a very obvious gap in the original firmware that had caused some to complain.

If you want to make sure that your iPhone doesn't change orientation when you're using it on the move, you can lock it in one orientation by double-clicking the home button to call up the task manager, swiping right to bring up the controls and tapping the orientation lock button on the far left of the bar (see below).

Copy, cut and paste

Copy, cut and paste were late arrivals in iOS, finally arriving in version 3. It's well implemented, though, and using them is easy: hold down your finger on a word you want to copy and, when you lift off, a selection box appears. Pick Select or Select all, and then drag the sliders to refine your selection. When you are happy with the selection, pick Copy or Cut from the menu. Now, if you want to paste, hold down for a second or two on the screen at the point where you want to paste and pick Paste from the pop-up menu.

Security

Before we go any further, a word about security. The iPhone has a voracious appetite for information. Contacts, addresses, bookmarks, notes, text messages… you name it, it will store it, and that's an awful lot of information to fall into an identity thief's hands if you happen to lose your handset.

Keeping your data secure

Add an extra layer of security by applying the iPhone's built-in locks, through Settings > General > Passcode lock. Tapping this will let you enter a four-digit code that will be demanded every time you or anyone else switches on the phone. With 10,000 combinations to choose from – assuming you count 0000 in your calculations – you shouldn't pick something too obvious such as your year of birth, your anniversary or the last four digits of your phone number. Once you have entered the number and confirmed it, you'll be asked to enter it every time you turn on the phone.

You can also set it, through the Require Passcode button, to lock the iPhone after one, five, 10, 15, 30 or 60 minutes, or four hours of inactivity and demand the code before it will work again, preventing anyone from browsing your data should you have the iPhone stolen.

You haven't entirely disabled your phone if you forget your code: you can recover it by connecting it to iTunes

and clicking Restore. This will return the iPhone to the state in which it left the factory and erase all of your data.

However, for some users a four-digit passcode simply isn't enough. Apple calls this four-digit string a Simple Passcode. To switch to a more comprehensive security model, tap the Simple Passcode switch to turn it off and, after entering your passcode once more, you'll be asked to supply a new, more complex code, which can use numbers, letters and special characters such as $, # and @. Choose this carefully and it will be close to impossible for anyone to guess.

By default, anyone who comes across your iPhone is given unlimited opportunities to guess your passcode. However, if you keep sensitive information in your handset then you should consider applying the Erase Data function, found at the bottom of the Passcode Lock settings, which will erase all data from your phone after ten unsuccessful attempts.

Choose a four digit code to secure your iPhone and you can keep your data safe from prying eyes, even if your handset is lost or stolen.

Resetting your iPhone

If you should forget your Passcode, all is not lost – you can still use your iPhone, although not without losing all of your data. By plugging it into your Mac or PC and starting iTunes, you can click the iPhone in the sidebar and then click Restore to delete all of the data on your phone and reinstate its factory settings.

This will delete all of your contacts, emails, account details, calendar appointments, photos, music and applications. If you use a Passcode it is therefore more important than ever to make sure you make regular backups of your device.

iPhone privacy

Privacy is becoming an ever hotter issue as people realise how easy it is to be tracked in our increasingly connected world. iOS therefore introduces a number of privacy controls that can be used to monitor how your data is being used.

Tap Settings > Privacy to see which parts of your stored data are in use by other applications. iOS 6 breaks down your data into categories, and organises each application that can access each type into related groups. So, tap Contacts or Calendars and you'll see which applications can access your address book and appointments. Tap Photos and iOS will pull up a list of applications with access to your photo roll. You can switch off authorised applications on a case-by-case basis by tapping the ON/OFF sliders beside each one.

The Location Services entry at the top of the list shows you which applications can reference your current position and thus potentially track your location. For this reason, the app-by-app sliders are supplemented by one master switch that lets you disable Location Services altogether.

It's up to you whether or not you set your iPhone to automatically wipe itself after a set number of incorrect attempts at entering your set passcode.

How to set a more secure passcode

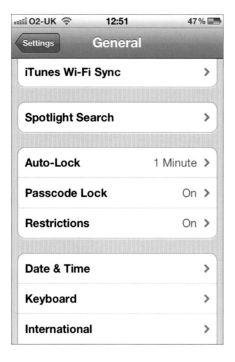

Step 1

Enter Settings and tap General > Passcode Lock. The status indicator beside the Passcode Lock line tells you whether or not you already have a lock in place. If not, your phone can be used by anyone who picks it up, just by switching on and swiping the screen.

Step 2

If you already have a passcode lock in place, you'll need to enter it before you can go any further. This ensures you are authorised to change settings on the phone. Various other settings on the phone employ the same security protocol to prevent casual users making changes.

Step 3

By default, your iPhone uses the Simple Passcode, which requires only four digits to unlock the handset. To set a more secure Passcode, tap the slider beside Simple Passcode to switch it off. None of these slider switches actually need to be slid in iOS to change their status.

Step 4

You can now enter a more secure password. Be careful when typing it to watch the screen and make sure that the last character entered, which is displayed at the end of the row of dots each time, is correct, as it will quickly disappear so that nobody can see it over your shoulder.

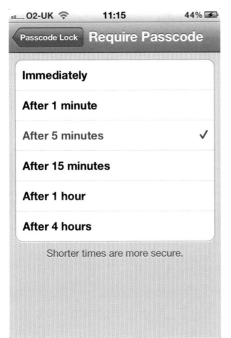

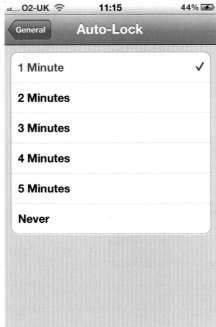

Degrees of security

The passcode is set to kick in automatically after a set period of time. It's up to you how long you let your iPhone stay unlocked for. You'll find this option through Settings | General | Passcode Lock | Require Passcode.

You should carefully balance the length of the passcode delay so that you maintain a good degree of security by setting it to kick in quickly enough while also not inconveniencing yourself by forever having to type in your code. We have found five minutes to be a happy medium, but it is good to get into the habit or changing this from time to time depending on your circumstances.

Enabling Auto-Lock

As well as requiring the passcode at set intervals you should set Auto-Lock to kick in when you are not using your iPhone.

You can safely set this to a shorter interval than the Require Passcode measurement as it won't require the passcode to re-enable your phone once it has been activated.

The Auto-Lock puts your iPhone into standby, thereby saving energy by shutting down some processes and turning off the screen, which is one of the biggest drains on its battery. If you set your iPhone to never invoke Auto-Lock you will need to remember to manually sleep it by pressing the power switch.

Privacy and Do Not Disturb

On the face of it, you might think that security and privacy are one and the same, but not where your iPhone is concerned. Security deals with the physical and digital wellbeing of your device, stopping other people from using it and recovering it when it's been lost or stolen. Privacy has more to do with specifying when you do and don't want to be disturbed, and what exceptions – if any – there are to these rules.

Avoiding distractions

It's always been possible – since the arrival of the very first iPhone – to flip a switch on the side of the handset to mute the ringer when you don't want it to sound. This is particularly useful when you're riding in a quiet coach on the train, or visiting a location, such as a church or museum, when a ringing phone would attract some frowns. However, with iOS 6 you can go much further, courtesy of a fully-fledged Do Not Disturb feature (see Settings | Do Not Disturb).

Switching this on prevents calls and texts from sounding any alerts when they reach your phone, so while you'll still be able to make outgoing calls and send texts yourself, and it will receive incoming messages, it will act as though it's switched off in the incoming direction (see *right*). It also silences any application alerts that might fire, such as Twitter and Facebook updates or incoming emails.

Switching on Do Not Disturb silences all notifications on your phone so you can get a good night's sleep.

At its most basic, Do Not Disturb is a simple on or off option, but by digging a little deeper you can customise it.

Tap Notifications | Do Not Disturb to open its options if you want to take things further. Here, you can schedule the Do Not Disturb feature to kick in automatically during certain hours of the day. This would be useful for anyone who works shifts and wouldn't want people calling them during the day if they were sleeping.

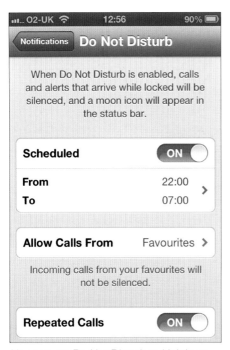

You can set Do Not Disturb to kick in at scheduled times, and make exceptions for important callers.

However, it can be just as useful for anyone who shouldn't be disturbed from their work, such as a teacher standing at the front of a classroom who naturally won't want to have their phone ringing in the presence of students who have been told that this is a sign of disrespect.

You'll notice that when it's active the feature puts a moon icon beside the clock, regardless of the time of day, to indicate that it's active.

iOS 6 recognises that there are times when it's important certain people can still get through, even if your phone is set to this mode. For example, you may be a parent whose children have locked themselves out of the house, or you may be caring for a sick relative who needs to call on you at short notice.

In these instances you would set the iPhone to allow through calls from a particular group in your Contacts list. By default it is anyone who has been set as a Favourite, but you can alternatively change this to any defined group. So, you could trim down the list yet further by organising just close family members into a new list and setting that as the only group of people who can break the Do Not Disturb rule.

If even this would be too much, tap Settings | Notifications | Do Not Disturb | Allow Calls From and select No One.

The final option is to decide how your iPhone should handle repeated calls.

iOS 6 considers any call that comes in from the same number in three minutes or less to be a repeated call, and it's set to let these through regardless of whether or not your iPhone is set to Do Not Disturb (even if you've set Allow Calls to No One).

The logic here is that anyone who urgently needs to speak to you is more likely to call you again right away rather than leave a message. Again, you can disable this by tapping the ON/OFF slider beside Repeated Calls.

Mail

Apple learnt a lesson from the BlackBerry when it was developing the iPhone: users like email on the move. And like the best students, Apple went out into the world and did better than its teacher.

Email on the iPhone is far from a weak point. It has presets for Gmail (Google Mail), Yahoo!, iCloud, AOL, Hotmail and Exchange, and also lets you manually add a regular Pop3 or Imap account from another provider. This last option, along with Exchange, will be of particular interest to business users, as it allows messages to be hosted on a central server rather than downloaded on an ad-hoc basis and deleted. iCloud works in much the same way, allowing you to see your in- and out-boxes in the same state on an iPhone, Mac or PC, or through a web browser.

Adding your first email account

If you don't already have an email account that you would like to use with your iPhone, you can set up a free account with five of the pre-set services in the iPhone's mail application by visiting the following sites using a regular web browser (not an email client):

iCloud	www.icloud.com
Yahoo! Mail	www.ymail.com
AOL Mail	www.aol.com
Google Mail	www.google.com/mail
Hotmail	www.hotmail.com

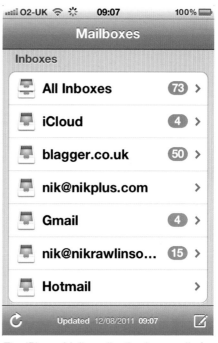

The iPhone Mail application keeps all of your accounts in one place.

However, by far the most useful for any iPhone user is iCloud, which provides you with a push email account. This transfers messages to the iPhone as soon as they are received, mimicking the BlackBerry's way of working, and saving you from having to manually invoke a collection. It also provides you with a wholly memorable @me.com email address and can be used with other services such as iTunes Match and Find My iPhone to provide additional features.

Picking up messages

When first set up, your email will be set to only pick up when you tell it to. This is great for making sure you rule your messages, rather than allowing them to rule you, but it's not entirely convenient.

To set your iPhone to poll the server and download new messages automatically, tap Settings > Mail, Contacts, Calendars > Fetch New Data and choose from every 15, 30 or 60 minutes, depending on how much of an email junkie you are. Checking more frequently can run down your battery

more quickly. Of course, if you're waiting for an urgent message you can still check manually from the Mail application by dragging down the message list so that the most recent entry pulls away from the top of the screen (see grab, below). Once you have picked up your messages, you will naturally sort through them, reading them, replying to the ones that need immediate action, and postponing others. A lot of messages can be deleted right away, which you can do by tapping the Bin icon at the bottom of the screen, at which point the message will sweep down into the bin.

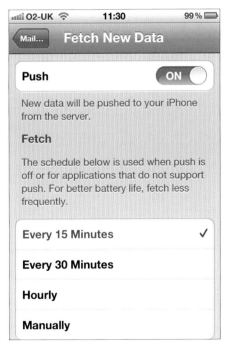

Stay in control of your email: choose the intervals at which it should be collected.

Dragging down your mail list further than the top message updates from the server.

Others will need some thought, and so naturally you will want to mark them as unread or flag them for following up. To do this, and with the email open on your iPhone screen, tap the flag on the toolbar and select Mark as Unread (see below).

Sending messages

You can send a message from anywhere in the Mail application without having to return to the main mailbox screen, by clicking the small square and pencil icon in the bottom right-hand corner. If you already know the address of the person you want to message you can type it straight in, but it is easier to tap the blue '+' icon to the right of the To field and select the person from your contacts list where youll be given the chance to pick the appropriate address if they have more than one in their record.

The procedure for replying to messages that you are reading is the same as above, except that instead of tapping the square and pencil icon, you tap on the backwards-pointing arrow, which would give you the option of either forwarding or replying to the presently-displayed message (*right*).

The flag icon on the Mail toolbar lets you mark messages you want to read later.

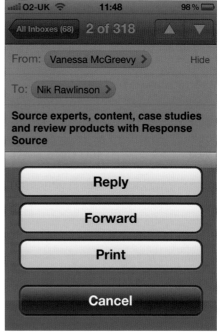

Tap the curled arrow to access Mail's reply and forward commands

Setting an email signature

You should set a signature to appear at the foot of every email. Despite appearing below the body of your message, this is the digital equivalent of headed note paper, giving you an opportunity to promote your website or, in the case of many businesses, to position a legal disclaimer.

To do this tap Settings > Mail, Contacts, Calendars > Signature (below) and choose whether you want one single signature for all accounts, or a separate one for each. It is good practice to

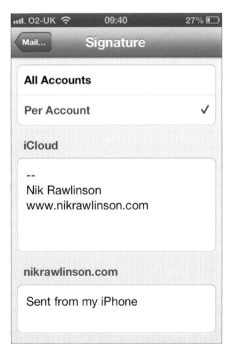

iOS 6 lets you set your email signature on an account-by-account basis.

precede your signature with two dashes and a space ('-- ') and then start the footer on the next line down. In this way, most email clients will trim it off when your message is quoted back to you in a subsequent email and both save on bandwidth use and prevent your details being passed on.

Managing messaging defaults

Several iPhone features, such as emailing video links from YouTube or jottings from the Notes tool, will always use your default email address to dispatch messages. The default address is whichever one you set up first. If you have set up several accounts and would like one of your later additions to work as the default, and so handle email from other iPhone applications, change it through Settings > Mail, Contacts, Calendars > Default Account.

VIP mailbox

New in iOS 6 is the VIP mailbox, which lets you specify which if your contacts are of higher priority than the others so that you can get to their messages without wading through a deluge of other incoming emails.

After adding contacts to your VIP list you can use the VIP settings in the centralised Settings app to change the way that notifications handle the arrival of email from these contacts, optionally detting a different email notification tone so you know now to hurry to check your mail if you hear anything else.

Safari

Safari is the iPhone's web browser. By default it is found on the Dock so that it appears on every home screen – that's how important it is. As with a Mac or PC, you can swap it out for an alternative, such as the excellent Chrome, from Google, but you can't ever make an alternative browser your default your default browser. That means that any links you open from web pages or other applications will always be sent to Safari.

If you use Safari on the Mac or PC, many of its controls and interface elements will already look familiar. The toolbar that runs across the bottom of the screen has your forward and back controls, a button for opening new browser windows, the bookmark manager (it looks like an open book) and the shortcut saver (the box with an arrow coming out of it). At the top of the screen are two input boxes: one for the web addresses you want to visit and the other for entering search terms that you want to send to Google. To date, Apple hasn't adopted a unified search and address bar here the way it has in Safari 6 on the Mac, which does away with the stand-alone search box.

When you first fire up Safari, it's set to use Google for its search results. It references the main .com version of the size, and although you can't change this to a localised national version you can switch away from Google wholesale if you choose, picking from either Yahoo! or

Bing as alternatives by tapping Settings > Safari > Search Engine.

In common with many other iPhone applications, and the version of Safari that ships with OS X, this mobile edition does an excellent job of recognising the dimensions of both your page and the elements positioned on it. Turn it to portrait or landscape orientation and you'll see that it resizes the content to fit the width of the screen, allowing you to choose between a wider, larger display, or a taller display that shows you more of every page. It also knows the dimensions of everything on the page so that double-tapping any element, such as a column of text, zooms the content until that element takes up the whole width of the screen, whichever way up you have it. You can now perform the same on the desktop by double-tapping a trackpad on any Mac running Safari 5 or later.

Reading view

Good though Safari's automatic resizing of content is when you dounle-tap like that, there are times when you simply don't need all of the content on a page that's surrounding what you're trying to read. Neither do you need the adverts and banners that appear above, below and within the page.

At times like this you can strip them out by switching to the Reader view, which isolates the main body content and presents just that, free of ads and distractions. Rather cleverly, it also recognises when a story spreads itself across several pages and stitches them all together so that you can scroll straight through the content without having to click from one page to another.

The Reader view is invoked by tapping the button marked 'Reader' next to the page address in the URL bar (see left). When you've finished reading, tapping Done returns you to the original page. In the meantime, dedicated controls in the Reader view let you change the font size and share the stripped-out content by email and over social networks, copy it or send it to a printer.

Emailing a web page's contents in this way is a more efficient way to bring it to your contacts' attention as the Reader view sends the content of the page in the body of the email, complete with a link back to the source and a selection of styled fonts and embedded graphics. Be careful when emailing content from someone else's website to observe any usage restrictions, including copyright.

Searching Safari

All of Safari's controls are clustered on the toolbar, with many of the buttons sporting pop-up dialogues that reveal hidden features. Tap on the address box and start typing in the URL of the page you want, and a list of matching addresses you have recently visited will drop down so you can pick the one you want without typing the whole address. Likewise, start typing in the search box and it will drop down a list of suggestions from Google or your chosen alternative if you've set one through Settings and, below the list, any searches you have recently performed that match what you have typed so far.

The search box also intelligently searches the page you are currently browsing. Simply type in the term you want to find on the page, and the search results will show you how many times it appears on the current page. Scroll up the list of results until you reach the very bottom entry and tap the search term under the 'On This Page' bar.

This switches you back to your page and highlights the first match for your search term in yellow (see right). Using the left and right arrows to the right of the toolbar steps you backwards and forwards through the remaining matches, with a counter at the centre showing which match you're currently viewing. Stepping forwards or backwards beyond the last or first match loops the page so that you return to the next hit at the start or end of the list.

How to add bookmarks to the iPhone Home screen

While it isn't exactly difficult to find your favourite pages in a regular list of bookmarks, it makes sense to save your most-used links to your iPhone Home screen, at which point they will launch like applications, without the Safari location toolbar in view and feel much more like a dedicated application.

The Search box also lets you hunt out specific phrases on the page you're currently reading. Each one is highlighted in yellow, with the buttons on the toolbar at the foot of the display stepping you forwards and backwards through them.

[1] Navigate to the page you want to link to and tap the shortcut button on the toolbar. This brings up the standard list of Safari controls, many of which – such as Twitter, Message, Mail and Facebook, are shared with other apps. Tap Add to Home Screen (see below) to save the link as a with a dedicated icon.

[2] If the site doesn't have its own dedicated icon, Safari will create one using a thumbnail from the webpage itself. However, developers can create their own, and your iPhone will respect this and use it in place on the home screen if it exists. All you need to do is give it a name that will make it easy to recognise among your applications.

[3] Your link will be added to your home screen and to all intents and purposes acts just like any regular application link, which means that if you find you are using it frequently you can drag it to the Dock.

[4] To remove a link from the Home screen, hold your finger on it until the icons start to shiver and each sprouts a small 'x' in a circle. Tap this and then confirm that you want to delete the bookmark.

Be careful when removing saved links in this way as no backup is stored in your regular bookmarks. If you want to set one, first tap the link to open it, save the bookmark and only then delete the icon.

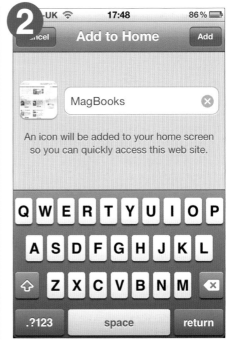

Reading List

Reading List was introduced in iOS 5, alongside an equivalent feature on Mac OS X Lion. It was improved in iOS 6 and Mountain Lion (OS X 10.8).

Recognising that we all have far busier lifestyles now, Apple has implemented this tool, which allows us to keep a note of pages we want to come back to when we have more time.

To mark a page in your Reading List, click the action button on the toolbar below your browser window (the curved arrow leaping out of a box) and select Add to Reading List. The page will be stored in the Reading List section of the regular Safari bookmarks, as shown below. Tapping the Reading List entry opens up the list of links.

The same feature appears in Safari on the Mac and PC, where a pair of glasses on the Bookmarks toolbar lets you save a page in the sidebar.

If you've signed up for a free iCloud account you can set it to synchronise your Reading List entries automatically, so that whichever device you are using when you have some free time to catch up on what you've missed, the List will be waiting.

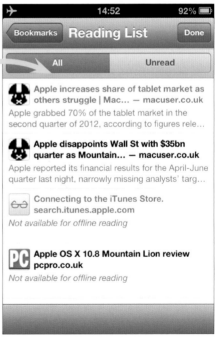

The really smart part of Reading List is that in the latest update it not only keeps track of the pages you have marked, but downloads their contents, too, so that even if you don't have network coverage – perhaps because you're in an area with poor propogation, or you're on a flight with your iPhone in Airplane Mode – you can still read the content of the saved pages from the Safari cache.

In the picture on the right on the opposite page, the first two articles in the list have been saved to the cache, along with a short preview, allowing them to be read whenever is most convenient.

iCloud tabs

Although it can perform other functions, like help you find a lost iPhone, iCloud is primarily focused on one thing: synchronisation. It's not surprising, then, to see Apple introduce the concept of iCloud tabs in iOS 6 and OS X Mountain Lion.

Quite simply, iCloud tabs synchronise your open pages between your various devices, so that if you were reading an online report on your Mac before leaving work it would be ready for you to carry on reading on your iPhone or iPad during your commute home. You wouldn't need to email a link to yourself or save it as a bookmark on any of your devices for this to work. In iOS, anything open on another iOS device, or a Mac, appears in the list under iCloud tabs. On the Mac, tabs open on other devices are displayed on a drop-down dialogue box attached to the toolbar.

If you have all the necessary kit and are updated to the latest versions of iOS, OS X and Safari, and still find that iCloud tabs isn't working for you, check that it's enabled on each of your devices. On the Mac, open System Preferences > iCloud and check that Bookmark syncing is active. On your iPhone, go to Settings > iCloud and check that the slider beside Safari is set to ON.

Sadly, iCloud tabs is a Mac-only feature as Apple didn't ship a version of Safari 6 for Windows at the same time as it released the OS X edition.

Podcasts

Apple launched its dedicated Podcasts app shortly before shipping iOS 6, and when the new operating system was released to the general public it completed the process of removing podcasts from iTunes and transitioning everyone over to the new app.

It works in a very similar way to iBooks and Newsstand, with an integrated store giving you access to an extensive library of podcasts ready to download for free.

Podcasts are recorded programmes, originally put out by amateurs but now widely adopted by professional broadcasters like the BBC, too. The vast majority are audio-only, but there's a good selection – often called vodcasts – that also incorporate video.

The easiest way to get started with podcasts is to browse the Top Stations tab (tap this on the bottom toolbar) by dragging the subject areas at the top of the screen left and right to choose one. Each brings up a whole column of different podcasts that you can choose from by scrolling the column up and down (see image, below left). Tap the switch at the top to choose audio or video.

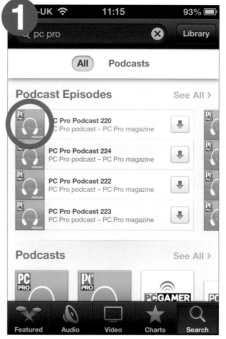

Subscribing to a podcast

[1] Tap the Catalogue button to enter the podcasts store and then use the search box to enter a keyword, broadcaster or the name of a podcast that you want to listen to. The app calls up a list of results in much the same way that the iBookstore lists matches to your searches there.

Tap the icon beside any episode to call up the full details, including reviews, ratings and a list of related podcasts that you might find interesting.

[2] Tap the arrow beside an episode to download it to your iPhone. When it arrives it will be organised in your podcast library, which you can find by tapping the

Podcasts button on the toolbar, beside Top Stations. Tap a podcast in this view to open the individual episodes.

[3] Tap an episode to listen to it, or tap the podcast thumbnail at the top of the details screen to access its settings.

From here you can choose whether or not you want to subscribe to the podcast on an ongoing basis, in which case your iPhone will automatically download new episodes as they become available, and how they should be organised in your library. By default it sorts them with the newest at the top of the list, which is the most logical. Scrolling down from here, you can also mark all episodes either as played or unplayed.

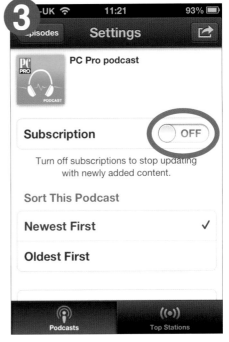

Passbook

Passbook is brand new in iOS 6. It's a simple idea: rather than having different loyalty apps installed on your iPhone, each handling different tickets, cards and vouchers, third-party developers can hook up their data to Passbook and it will all be displayed in one place.

It's a bit like Newsstand. When the iPad first launched and developers – and publishers – worked out that it was a viable alternative to printed publications, they rushed out a raft of digital mags. Each one was a separate application, and subscribing to several meant that you would have an application for each littering your home screen. Apple decided to tidy things up by introducing Newsstand, which gave them all a dedicated folder in which to reside.

Passbook does the same for tickets and vouchers, and gives iPhone users a single place to turn when they want to access their digital airline ticket, concert pass, coffee chain loyalty card and so on. Each will contain various details about the offer, credit balance or ticket terms and conditions, and can include a barcode or QR code that can be scanned when you use the ticket or pass, so there's no need to mess around with paper and card any more.

Passbook is location-aware, so if knows when you're passing a cinema for which you have a ticket, and throws up your ticket on the lock screen, ready for you to wave at the staff at the cinema

door. It can also be updated in real time, so if you've checked in for your flight using a digital ticket stored in your Passbook and the gate changes while you're drinking coffee in the terminal building, Passbook can update your virtual boarding card to show you where you need to be, and when.

For Passbook to be a success will rely on third-party developers embracing it in preference to their own stand-alone apps. Some may be reluctant to do this because they would see it as watering down the visibility of their brand on an extremely important platform, but the speedy adoption of Newsstand suggests Apple could well be on to something here – particularly if users grow to rely on it.

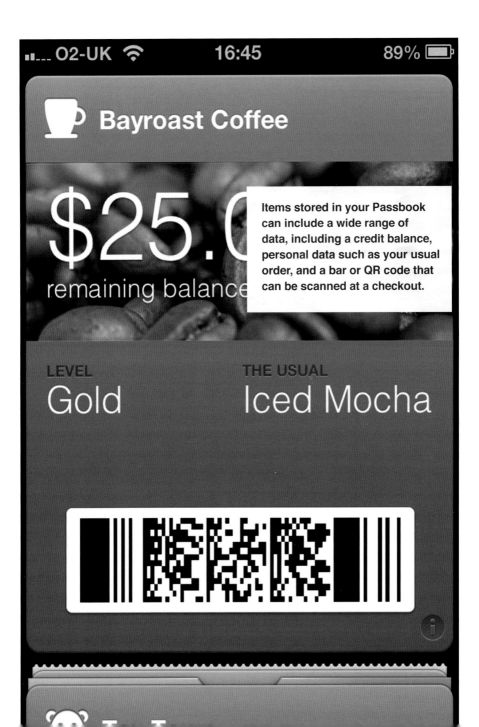

Items stored in your Passbook can include a wide range of data, including a credit balance, personal data such as your usual order, and a bar or QR code that can be scanned at a checkout.

Adding passes to Passbook

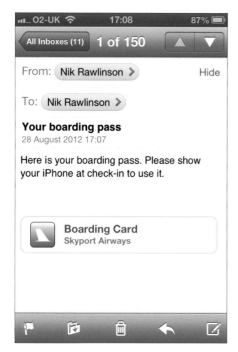

Retailers can provide you with a pass in any number of ways, including through installed apps or direct downloads. One of the easiest ways to send a pass is by email, however. This would allow third-parties to email a pass directly to a customer when they fill out an online form, and thus simultaneously confirm that their email address is valid.

When the pass arrives it will be appended to the email like a regular attachment, with an appropriate logo and a line describing what it is. Adding it to the Passbook is a simple matter of tapping the pass in the body of the email, at which point a preview will appear on the following screen, including whatever information the retailer has chosen to include. Tapping the 'i' in the corner flips it around to display supplementary information such as terms and conditions or, in the case above, passport details relating to the passenger to whom the ticket has been sold.

Assuming there are no problems with the pass and all of the details are correct, tap the Add button at the top of the interface to file it away in Passbook.

Managing passes in Passbook

Over time you'll find that some of your passes are no longer relevant.It could be that a loyalty card has run out of credit, you've moved away from a local shop to an area that doesn't have another outlet, or you've used a transport or entertainment ticket that can't be re-used.

On those occasions you'll want to delete expired passes from your Passbook so that it doesn't get cluttered.

To do this, open the pass and then tap the 'i' in the lower corner to flip it around, followed by the trash can icon at the top of the screen. After you've confirmed

that you really want to remove the pass permanently it will be run through a virtual shredder, and when you return to the Passbook overview screen it will have disappeared from your wallet.

The back side of your passes is also where you can perform a couple of management tasks, including specifying whether they should appear on the Lock Screen (in which case they can pop up in specific geographic locations) and whether they should update automatically, such as when your airline is switched to an alternative gate.

Reminders

Reminders is a deceptively simple application. At first glance it appears to be nothing more than a simple list taker, giving you somewhere to jot down thoughts and reminders so that you don't need to worry about forgetting them.

Dig deeper, though, and you'll see that it's actually far more accomplished.

Reminders lets you set deadlines, as you would expect, by which your jobs must be completed. However, it recognises that not all tasks can be performed to a set deadline, as some must be conducted at a particular location. To this end, you can set reminders on the basis of position, rather than time. Here, we'll show you how.

1. Fire up Reminders and start adding notes. Use the '+' button at the top of the interface to start work on your first one, and press Return at the end of entering each one. This immediately takes you to the next line so you can start entering the next one without tapping '+' again. Tap anywhere else on the interface after entering your last one.

2. Let's start adding some deadlines. Tap the Back up computer task, followed by the ON/OFF slider beside On a Day, then use the tumblers to select a date and time by which the job must be done.

3. Backing up your computer is a very important job, so we'll give it a priority,

too. Tap Done to return to the main settings page, followed by More and Priority. Select High from the list of options.

4. Before we can back up our computer we need to make sure we have sufficient storage, so we'll buy a new hard drive. We can remind ourselves that we need to do this without creating a whole new reminder on the main screen by tapping within the Notes field and tapping in our reminder.

5. We've completed the first step in building ourselves a working list of tasks. Tap Done to return to the overall Reminders list and you'll see that we have now set deadlines for the two jobs. We'll now go on to create a geographic reminder for buying cheese.

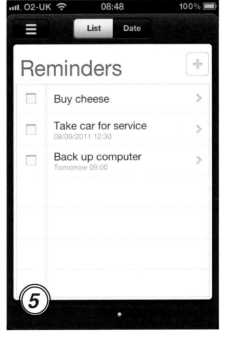

Adding geographical reminders

Some jobs can only be performed in a particular location, and for them a date and time-based reminder may not be appropriate. Reminders therefore lets you set a location relevant to the job, and will then use the iPhone's built-in.GPS features to remind you to perform the job when you arrive at or leave the location in question. Here we'll add a place-based reminder to the cheese-buying job.

1. You can only set reminders for locations that have been saved to your address book contacts list. We need to be reminded to buy cheese when we get to the supermarket, which naturally isn't one of our personal contacts. The first step, then, is to add it to the address book. Do this by searching for it in the Maps application. When you have located it, tap the blue arrow at the end of the location pop-up marker.

2. This calls up the location's publicly available information, drawn from various directory sources. To save us adding it to the address book manually we can simply tap the Add to Contacts at the bottom of its address card.

3. Return to the Reminders application and tap the Buy cheese entry, followed by Remind Me. This time, instead of tapping the ON/OFF slider beside On a Day, tap the one beside At a Location. The location box will expand below it to show that currently it is set to remind you at home – your present location. This is no good,

so tap Home to pick a more relevant spot an then tap Choose Address on the next screen.

4. Scroll through your address book, use its search tool or navigate your existing groups to find the location you saved in step 2. Here we have located Sainsburys Springfield in the S section of our address book. We only need to tap it once to add it to the Reminder.

5. Tap the Remind Me button to step back to the previous screen. At present the reminder is still set to trigger when you leave the location as this was relevant for when you were setting reminders relating to your home location. Tap When I Arrive, and then Done. Reminders will now monitor your location and pop up an alert when you're passing the supermarket.

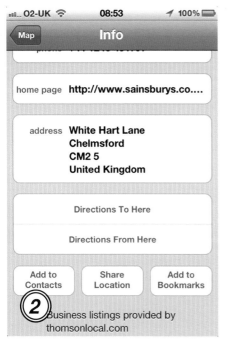

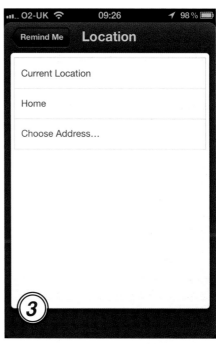

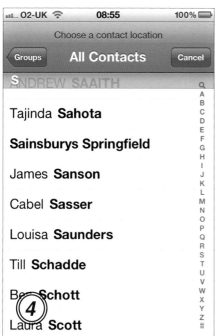

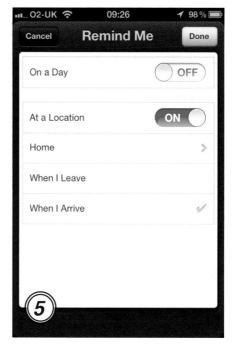

Music

The iPod app is no more. That's no bad thing, as the idea of the iPod being relegated to the status of mere software was a bit humbling. In its place we now have 'Music', which bears more than a striking similarity to its predecessor. There is one big change from pre-iOS 5 versions, though – the absence of movies and TV shows, which have been hived off into a dedicated app called Video.

If you used the old iPod app then you'll find Music immediately familiar. The menubar at the bottom of the screen lets you slice and dice your music library in

whichever way makes the most sense to you, with presets for playlists (which can be imorted from your Mac or PC), artists, songs and albums.

Drag down any of these categories and you'll reveal a search box hiding at the top of the listing *[1]*. Type into this and the results list will update in real time to show only matching albums or tracks.

Tap on the Songs entry and you can scroll through all of the tracks on your iPhone *[2]* or, more importantly, tap the Shuffle button that appears at the top of the list to play everything in random order.

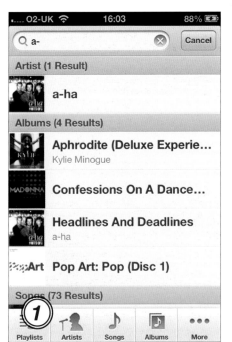

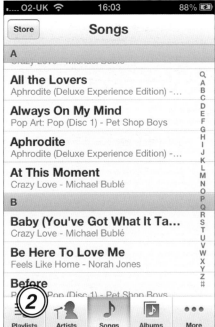

You can also shuffle within an album if you open it first *[3]*, which is often enough to give a new breath of life to something you're starting to tire of.

On opening an album you'll be presented with a list of the tracks it comprises, allowing you to go straight to the one you want to listen to, at which point the listing will spin around to display the full album art *[4]*.

To return to the listing while the album is playing, tap the icon in the top right corner of the display to ftemporarily flip around the cover art.

Shared playlists

If you're using your iPhone at home or work, where you also keep your regular iTunes library, enable Home Sharing on both your iPhone and your Mac or PC. You'll then be able to play your full library on your iPhone without syncing it to your mobile device.

Obviously you need to be using iTunes on either a Mac or PC to be able to do this, but once it's set up it means that your complete music collection will be available on all of your devices.

To share a library, open iTunes on your regular computer and click iTunes > Preferences... > Sharing on the Mac, or Edit > Preferences > Sharing on the PC.

Check the box beside Share my library on my local network. Your library, complete with its playlists, will then appear in the sidebar of any other installation of iTunes running on your network. By default, each user will see the whole of your library.

Despite sharing your library in this way, you retain a great degree of control over what can be seen within your library.

If you don't want to share the more embarassing sections of your iTunes library, you need only gather them into a dedicated playlist and click on the radio

button beside 'Share selected playlists', then check only the playlists you want to share – remembering to omit that embarassing collection of hidden tracks that you don't want to make public.

You can also restrict the people who are able to access any of your library by setting a password. This is particularly useful if you are running an older Mac that might become bogged down if too many other users start playing music – or TV shows and movies, which are also shared – from your computer.

To access the shared tracks, simply tap More on the toolbar, followed by Shared. Pick the name of your shared home library and all of its tracks will appear as though they were local.

Sharing your music library, so long as it's stored in an iTunes Library on your Mac or PC. It's possible to share only selected playlists if you want to keep some of your library to yourself (below). Once set up, they'll be broadcast on your local network so that your iPhone Music app can find them automatically (left).

How to build a playlist

Playlists let you gather together a collection of your favourite tracks, or tracks of a certain type such as Christmas music, and organise them in one sorted list so that you can always get to them without having to search for them or skip backwards and forward through individual entries in your library.

Building your own playlist is simple. Start by tapping the 'playlist' button on the Music toolbar at the bottom of the screen, then tap the Add Playlist... link. Music will ask for a name, so give it something memorable. *[1]*

Music switches to a view of the tracks in your library, each of which will now be accompanied by a '+' to the right of its name. Scroll through the list of tracks and tap the '+' relating to each track you want to add to the playlist. Each time you add a track it will be greyed out so that you know it is already on the playlist and you don't try to add it twice. When you have added all the tracks you want to use, tap the Done button to save the playlist. *[2]*

Music now shows a view of your playlist. From here you can immediately skip to a track you want to play, or tap Shuffle to play them all in a random order. Three buttons at the top of the list let you respectively edit the contents of the playlist, clear it out so that the playlist container is retained while the tracks in it are removed, or delete the playlist altogether. Note that the 'clear' and 'delete' options only remove the list parameters; they don't remove the tracks from your iPhone. *[3]*

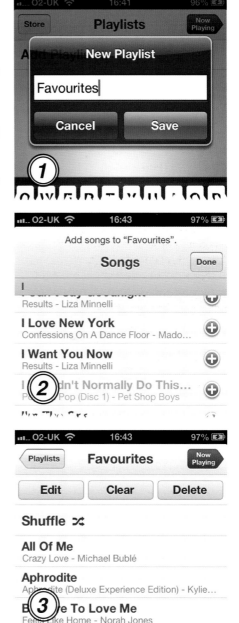

Music settings

Although Music's features are controlled through the app itself, many of its settings are controlled through the iPhone's centralised Settings app. Tap Settings > Music to find them. *[1]*

Several of these are on/off features, such as Shake to Shuffle, which picks another random track from your current playlist when you shake the iPhone. This is handy if you want to change tracks without having to navigate the menus, but do bear in mind that activating this feature opens the potential that your iPhone will skip to a different track if you head out jogging with it.

Some of the features, though, such as EQ *[2]*, open up a second-level menu from which you can pick a particular setting. EQ is an interesting option as it lets you change the way that your tracks sound on a global basis, with presets for particular music types, such as classical or dance, and others that emphasis particular parts of a track, such as the bass or treble.

It's also possible to limit the maximum volume at which the Music app will play back music from here, but it remains easy to disable this feature by stepping back into the setting and dragging the volume limit slider to a new position.

Parents who want to make sure that their children don't play their music too loud should therefore enable restrictions on their iPhones by tapping Settings > General > Restrictions, tapping the Enable Restrictions button and entering a four digit code to stop anyone else turning off the restrictions. When you've done that, scroll down to Allow Changes, tap Volume Limit and turn off the option to allow this to be changed. *[3]*

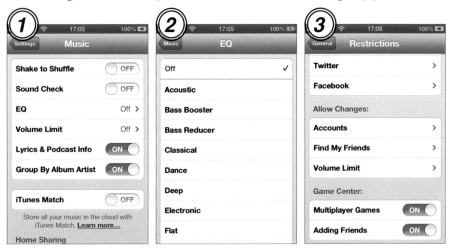

Videos

Videos is one of the simplest apps on the iPhone. Many of its features were at one time rolled into the now defunct iPod application, which itself was replaced by 'Music' when iOS 5 shipped. It didn't reappear in iOS 6.

Videos exists purely to play back downloads from the iTunes Store, or movies and TV shows you have synchronised through iTunes from your Mac or PC. Movies that you shoot yourself using the built-in camera on your iPhone are stored instead in your regular photo albums, while those that you edit with an application like iMovie are stored in the app itself until you synchronise or send them to a third-party online service, or actively choose to save them out to your Photo roll.

Your videos are organised into collections, with related episodes gathered into parent groups, each of which includes details of how many episodes it contains. You'll also see a small blue indicator beside the name of each episode showing whether a programme is new (filled in blue), partially watched (half-filled with blue) or watched right through (empty). The same indicator appears in the overview of each of your collections showing you how many of the constituent videos you still need to watch inside it.

Tap a video to start it playing and you'll immediately notice that this is one application that only works in one direction – landscape. Don't bother shaking your iPhone to get it to right itself; simply turn it on its side and enjoy the video full screen.

The controls are simple, and we've explored them more fully in the graphic over the page. If you have any familiarity with a regular DVD player then you'll already know what everything does.

Unfortunately there's no way to find related movies from the playback half of the app, as there was with the now defunct YouTube application, but if you step back to a list of TV shows inside any

Navigate the Videos app

Progress bar. Hold down on the spot and drag left and right to move through the video.

Aspect ratio. Tap to switch between full screen and original.

Transport controls to pause and skip videos. Hold down on back and forward for rewind and fast forward.

Volume slider. Drag the spot to change, or use the buttons on the side of your phone.

one of your collections you'll find a link to Get More Episodes... which takes you directly to the iTunes Store.

Apple maintains an extensive library of both films and TV shows in its store, which you can download directly onto your iPhone. With most series you can choose

standard and high definition videos, the latter of which cost more, and can buy either single episodes or a complete series. If you have got iCloud set up to synchronise your purchases, anything you buy on your iPhone will automatically appear on your Mac or PC.

Adding movies and TV shows to your library

You can buy movies and TV shows directly through the iTunes App, where you'll find dedicated Films and TV Programmes sections. Apple provides a range of recommendations on the home screen, but using the Search function will let you explore the library in more depth.

Each programme and film is accompanied by a description, episode run-down, viewer reviews and related content that you might also enjoy once you have finished the content you're buying. They will also have star ratings, if other viewers have provided them.

Once you've found the material you're interested in downloading, tap its thumbnail to open up the full listing. If you're looking at a film, you'll be able to play a preview clip to check that it's what you're after. If you're looking at a TV show and want to do the same, tap one of the episodes and you'll find the preview clip at the top of the screen.

You can often choose between high definition and standard definition content in both TV shows and films. You'll find Also Available in HD... and Also Available in Standard Definition... buttons at the bottom of their listings if that's the case. Tapping the buttons lets you switch between them and changes the price as appropriate (see right).

If you're contemplating viewing a film that you probably won't watch more than once, then rent it instead of buying it and save yourself some money.

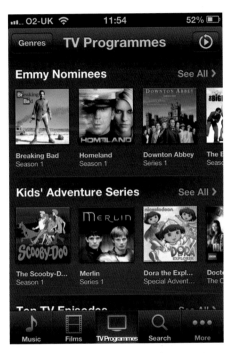

AirPlay

AirPlay is an extremely easy to use networking technology that makes it easy to direct audio and video around your home network. AirPlay compatible devices, such as Apple TV, AirPort Express and third-party speakers and Docks advertise their presence on the network so that they can be detected by the iPhone, iPad, iPod touch or Macs running iTunes (or any other application on OS X 10.8 Mountain Lion).

Once an application is connected to your network and plugged in, you only need to fire up one of the iOS audio or video apps to put it to use.

Here we're using Music, the app that replaced iPod in iOS 5 and 6 to stream an album over our home network to a set of speakers in a room downstairs from our iPhone.

We know that the iPhone has spotted the AirPort Express to which they are connected because it has displayed the AirPlay icon in the Music toolbar, beside the volume control (see the circled icon, below). Tapping this lets us select the output destination from the range of detected deviced on the network (see grab, right).

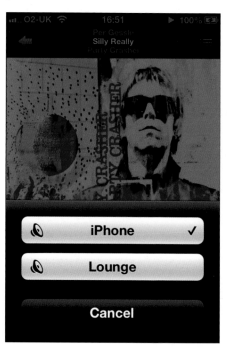

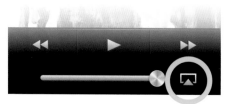

AirPlay looks for compatible speakers, AirPort Express and Apple TV boxes on your network with which to share media.

The full range of controls is still available through the iPhone, which means that we don't need to get up and walk over to the connected speaker to change the volume or change tracks. Dragging the slider on the iPhone's Music application changes the volume being fed to the speaker, and the regular transport controls (forwards, backwards and so on) still work on the iPhone the same way they would if you were using headphones.

Gum Plus™

The high-capacity, high-style backup battery

Just Mobile Gum Plus™ is a stylish portable backup battery for iPod, iPhone, iPad and USB-powered devices. The impressive 5,200 mAh power and 2,100 mAh output current can recharge your iPhone up to 3 times and juice it up to 90% in just an hour.

With its rounded aluminium case and five LED power indicators, the Gum Plus™ is a truly stylish way to pack a power up.

Love design?
Like Just Mobile

Newsstand

Apple's drive to become involved in every piece of content that appears on your iPhone now extends to newspapers and magazines, too.

Even before the arrival of iOS 5 it had changed the terms and conditions governing the applications sold through its Store for use on the iPhone and iPad to specify that magazines and paper updates counted as in-app purchases, just like credits and new levels in an iOS game. They therefore all have to be processed through Apple's own payments system, with Apple taking a 30% cut of the revenue. It makes sense, therefore,

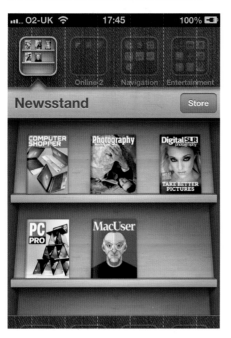

for Apple to also provide Newsstand, an application through which we can organise our subscriptions and buy new ones, just as we do with books through the iBooks application.

When you first fire it up, its shelves will be empty, but you can quickly fix that by tapping the Store button to visit the dedicated papers and magazine apps section of the iTunes Store, and from there start downloading some reading matter.

The clever part comes when your publications start to update their issues, at which point Newsstand will discreetly download new issues in the background for the duration of your subscription and arrange them on the shelves, just as it does with your downloaded books.

Industry support for Newsstand is very strong, with many major publishers selling each of their magazine brands through Apple's digital newsagency.

Shopping through Newsstand

Apple has already worked out how we like to shop, with its online app store having so far shipped more than 15 billion applications to iPhone, iPad and iPod touch users. Some of these applications were already magazine-based apps, in which the pages of the magazine were bundled together into a small package that makes navigation easy and frequently adds new features such as live video, audio tracks and photo galleries.

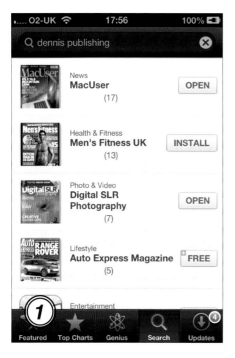

By moving this content into an app all of their own, iOS keeps our home screens from becoming cluttered and also makes it easier for us to find new content that interests us.

Payments will be made using your regular payment method – just as they are for books, apps, music and videos – and downloads will all take place in the background.

Watch out for notification badges appearing in the corner of the Newsstand application icon, which indicate when you have new content waiting to be read.

1. Open Newsstand from your home screen (you can't put it in a folder as it is technically just a specialised folder itself, so it will always be in view on one of your screens) and tap the Store button to visit the magazine store. Here you'll find Apple's selection of highlighted publications, just as you do with regular apps, and you can also use the search tool in the same way to find specific titles that aren't listed on the opening page.

2. Each publication app is just a container for the issues you will later download. You'll see a progress bar fill up as they download, and when it completes each one will be arranged on the Newsstand shelves so that you can see what you still need to read. Here we have downloaded the MacUser app, which gives us access to a comprehensive back catalogue.

85

3. Open one of the magazine apps you have just downloaded and you'll be asked to buy some content. The specific mechanics will vary from title to title, but in most cases you'll be able to sign up for a subscription or buy individual issues.

4. We've opted to buy a single copy of the current issue of MacUser magazine by tapping the price beside its name. We now need to enter our password to prove that we're authorised to buy content using this Apple ID, at which point the download will commence. Again, a progress bar will track its completion [5].

6. Our issue is here and ready to be read. Tap the library button (bottom left) and then tap View beside the downloaded issue. Swipe the pages left and right to move through the issue, double-tap to zoom in on the pages and single-tap to call up the menu. This shows you thumbnails of each spread so you can move through them more quickly.

7. Tap the three bulleted lines on the toolbar to call up the full list of contents and use the tumbler to scroll through them. When you find the one you want to read, tap View Article to read it.

8. Alternatively, if the headline of an article doesn't make it obvious where the item you're after can be found, tap the magnifier to call up the search box, and then enter a keyword. Each of the results in the corresponding list is accompanied by a thumbnail so you can quickly identify the page you need.

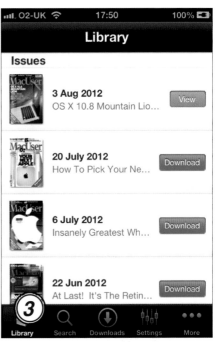

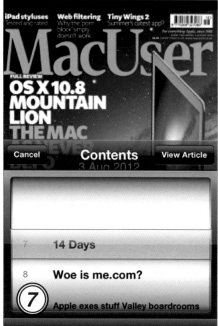

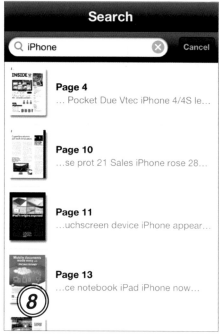

iMessage

iMessage is Apple's proprietary messaging system, designed to be used as a supplement to regular text and picture messaging on devices running iOS 5 and later. In effect, it adds a kind of text messaging feature to the iPod touch and iPad, neither of which had that feature before.

Before you can use it, you must enable iMessage by tapping Preferences | Messages, and then tapping the OFF/ON switch to activate the service. You then need to decide how people can contact you. They'll already be able to use your phone number, but not everyone will know that, although they may know your email address or Apple ID. You should therefore add them as valid destinations for your incoming messages.

Scroll down to the Send & Receive box and tap it, then start by tapping Use your Apple ID for iMessage. *[1]* You'll need to supply your password to authorise the service, and then tap Sign in. Once it has completed the process, you'll be able to add further email addresses to iMessage, so that even those people who don't know your Apple ID will still be able to find you.

If you add several contact options in this way you might find that iMessage sets one of your least-used addresses as the default originator of new conversations. *[2]* You can change this quite simply by scrolling further down the screen and picking an alternative in the Start new conversations from: panel.

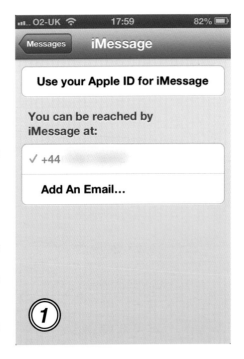

When you've finished setting it up, you can exit the iMessage preferences and start using the app itself..

You can now send iMessages directly by tapping on the Messages app on the home screen and typing in what you want to say, using your contact's email address or their phone number as the destination, or picking someone from your Contacts list. Some core apps in iOS 6 and iOS 5 also hook into iMessage as a conduit through which to send their contents. *[3]*

For example, open an image from the Photos app and tap the shortcut button

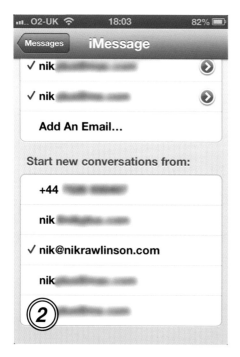

on the bottom toolbar (the curved arrow coming out of a rectangular box). Here you'll find an option for Message which, when tapped, drops your image into a new message with space above for you to write a covering note.

iMessages synchronise through iCloud so if you have several iOS devices you'll find the same stream on each of them. Further, because it works across Apple's own servers via either a wifi network or your 3G connection, any messages that you send are free and won't be deducted from your monthly contract.

iMessage vs SMS

Although they perform a very similar function, it's inconceivable that Apple would entirely remove SMS messaging from a future release of the iPhone. That's because – at present, at least – Apple devices are the only ones that can access iMessage content, and so it would cut off iOS-based handsets from the rest of the mobile phone-using population, which would make them immediately unpopular. Also unlikely would be Apple opening up iMessage, as it's a unique reason to buy.

iMessage works in a very similar fashion to SMS if all you want to do is send brief notes to your friends. However, if you want to go beyond this relatively simple means of communication it will quickly prove itself to be far more versatile.

As well as regular notes you can use it to send map links, or files from a variety of applications installed on your iPhone, such as the Photos application.

The full range of sharing methods open to any application will depend on its unique abilities and the kind of data it's handling, but Photos is one of the most versatile (see above left). Tap Message and enter your contact details by entering their name as it appears in your Contacts book (abobe right), or their number or email address. Tapping Send completes the process and dispatches the file to their own iMessage client.

If you have previously had any correspondence with this contact which you have not removed from your Messages history this latest posting will be added to the end of the existing message stream, with responses posted directly below it.

FaceTime

FaceTime is Apple's young but rapidly growing video conferencing tool. It appeared in iOS 4, the previous iteration of the iPhone operating system, and has now reached out onto OS X, the company's operating system for its Mac line of computers.

This extesion of the platform allows users with an iPhone, iPad, iPod touch or Mac (with suitable camera if they aren't using a portable Mac or iMac, which has the renamed FaceTime camera built in to the lid or the bezel of the screen) to talk to each other by video, in real time, without paying any call charges.

How to use FaceTime

FaceTime uses the Internet to patch together its users. Because of the amount of data that it needs to pass between the two participants to maintain a constant, smooth video stream, it took until the arrival of iOS 6 for it to be possible to make FaceTime calls over the 3G cellphone network. Note that doing so could have a serious impact on the amount of data you still have available to use from your monthly allowance for other browsing activities if you use FaceTime in this way on a regular basis.

To place a FaceTime call you need to have an Apple ID. If you are signed up to iCloud then you can use your login details for that service to access FaceTime. However, if you don't you can get yourself

a free ID at *https://appleid.apple.com/* or by signing up through the FaceTime preferences.

[1] FaceTime may be switched off on your iPhone, so the first thing you need to do is check that it is active. Open its preferences by launching the Setting app and tapping FaceTime. Check that the slider beside FaceTime is set to ON. If it isn't, tap it to wake it up.

[2] At this point FaceTime will probably be set to only send incoming calls to your

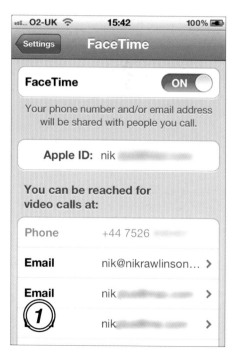

End

phone by way of your phone number, which as we explained in relation to iMessage might not be something that your contacts know. You should therefore add some extra contact methods to the system.

Start by tapping Use your Apple ID for FaceTime, and then provide your password to prove that you are authorised to add it to the system. Once it has been checked and verified, tap Next to step through to the next screen and then select which of your existing email addresses you want to allow people to contact you on through the system. By default it will show each of the addresses that you have already set up in the Mail application, but you can add new addresses that aren't already set up by tapping Add An Email...

[3] To make your own outgoing FaceTime calls you need to visit the Phone or Contacts apps as unlike OS X, iOS doesn't have a FaceTime app. If you're starting from the Phone app, tap Contacts to view the addresses in your contacts list. Find the card for the person you want to contact and scroll down to the bottom of their details. Here you'll find options to send messages, share that contact's details, add them to your list of favourite contacts or start a FaceTime call with them. Tap this and the screen will clear.

The front-mounted camera will now become active and your iPhone will initiate the call over your wireless network.

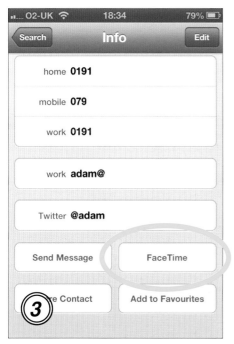

Assuming it's successful, your image will shrink to a small thumbnail in the corner of the screen so that you can see the other person's image more clearly. If you want to show them a view of what you can see in front of you, tap the spin button to switch to the rear camera.

[4] If you are already on a regular voice call with another FaceTime subscriber you can switch to using FaceTime in the middle of your conversation.

Not only would this enable you to see them so that you can each demonstrate something that can't be easily described over the phone, but as your call would then be rerouted over the Internet rather than your regular cellphone connection you would stop having to pay for it either financially or through a deduction in the number of available minutes remaining free to be used through the rest of the month.

To do this while making a call, use the dedicated FaceTime button on the call control panel to switch services.

Camera

The iPhone camera has improved over the various generations. That's a good job, too, as the original was a disappointing 2 megapixel affair that took fairly poor pictures compared to modern day standards.

Today's iPhones shoot images at resolutions high enough to print and hang on the wall. Many of the cleverest features, though, are bundled up in iOS.

The camera hardware

The iPhone includes two cameras – one at the back for taking high resolution images and another positioned on the front, beside the speaker. Why? For two reasons. First and foremost to take advantage of the FaceTime video conferencing application so that you can

talk to your friends using the forward-facing camera while viewing them on the screen, and second so that you can take self portraits. There was no forward-pointing camera on the iPhone 3G and earlier, so you had to try and guess both when you were properly framed and when your finger was poised over the shutter button. Since iOS 5 you can now use the volume up button to activate the shutter.

Options, options

The Options button at the top of the Camera interface is the only control you have over the mechanics of the application. It is home to just two options: whether or not you want to show grid lines on the live display to help with your composition, and whether to enable high

dynamic range imaging, which preserves detail in the extreme highlight and shadow areas of your image.

The grid lines option is useful for keeping your horizons straight, as well as showing you the power points where the lines intersect.

The most exciting new feature of the iOS 6 camera app also resides here: panorama. Enabling this and then tapping the shutter button lets you rotate the camera across the view in front of you to create an automatically stitched and colour-corrected wide-angle view of the scene before you covering up to 240 degrees. You can see an example below.

This feature works on the iPhone 4S, iPhone 5 and fifth-generation iPod touch, but not the iPhone 4, even if you update your device to iOS 6.

The Camera app allows you to enable HDR and display grid lines on the screen to help keep your horizons horizontal.

Aside from the options that are available to you when using the Camera app itself, there is one further option in the central Settings app.

If you have enabled the option to shoot HDR versions of your images, your iPhone doesn't magically enable a more sensitive sensor to capture a wider spectrum of colours and tones. All it does is manipulate what it has already captured to maximise the amount of information that can be drawn out of the saved data.

Because this can very occasionally result in some over-vivid colours, depending on shooting conditions, Apple recognises that you might want to step back to the original captured data and discard the manupulated alternative. It therefore saves two versions of any HDR image by default: the original and the edited version.

This shouldn't cause too many problems as the iPhone's capacity is such that it won't be filled up too quickly by all of these extra copies, but it does mean you'll have a lot of extra images to scroll through when you're playing them back, more to download to your computer and, potentially, more being uploaded to your Photo Stream, which could take you close to your 1000 image limit.

You can therefore opt to discard the original version of each image if you are happy just to keep the high dynamic range derivatives. To do this, tap Settings | Photos and scroll down to the HDR section. Tap the ON/OFF slider and set it to OFF and the duller original shots won't be saved to your internal storage or uploaded to iCloud for synchronisation.

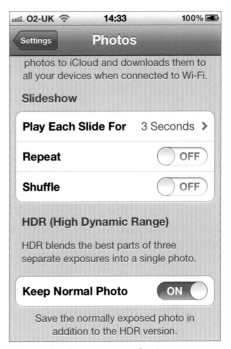

Turn to the iPhone's core Settings app to make further changes to the way the Camera's options perform.

Put your photos on the map

Every picture that you take is tagged with its location, courtesy of the iPhone's GPS chip and other geolocation features. This lets applications like Aperture and iPhoto, and photo sharing websites like Flickr, plot them on live maps.

The iPhone itself can also display your images on a map rather than simply in an Album. To see where your pictures were taken, open the Photos app and, from the toolbar on the albums screen, tap Places. Each is represented by a red push pin. Zoom in for more detail.

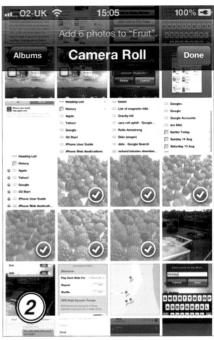

Organising your images

Your pictures are stored in albums that are accessible either by tapping the thumbnail on the camera icon, or through the dedicated Photos application. By default they are stored in a single album called Camera Roll.

This makes them easy to find but not easy to sort as they are organised in chronological order with thumbnails of each one scrolling down the screen in one large, unbroken list. Your videos are mixed in with them, too.

It therefore pays dividends to get into the habit of sorting your pictures into more appropriate albums as you take them. Here's how.

[1] Open the Photos app and, if you see your thumbnails, tap Album to step back to the overview. Tap Edit | Add and enter a logical name, then tap Save.

[2] You'll be returned to the Albums overview and need to add some photos to your newly-created album. Tap on your Camera roll to open it and scroll through the thumbnails until you find the ones for the photos that you want to add to the new album. Tap them in sequence and they'll be overlaid by a small tick. When you have selected all of the ones you want, tap Done to add them to your new album. Note that later deleting the album doesn't delete the images; they stay in your Camera Roll.

Twitter

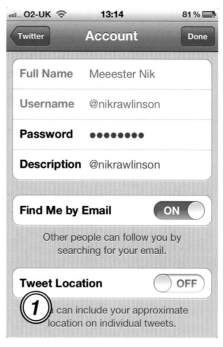

Twitter, the web-based messaging system that has taken the world by storm, is now a core feature of iOS on the iPhone and iPad. It's built in at the heart of the operating system, making it easier than ever to send short links and notes to your friends directly from inside some of the most important pre-installed applications.

Here we'll look at how you can add your Twitter account to your iPhone and send your first direct tweet.

[1] Tap Settings > Twitter to open the Twitter settings application and then start the process by tapping Add Account and entering your credentials. You can't actually sign up to Twitter through the Settings app, so if you don't already have an account of your own point a regular browser at *twitter.com* and join. It's free.

[2] Allow your iPhone to add Twitter contacts to the records in your address book. It does this by comparing your contacts' details with records already assigned to Twitter accounts and adding the Twitter usernames to any matching cards that it finds. It makes sense to repeat this process periodically to keep everything up to date.

[3] Authorise other iOS apps to use your Twitter account to post updates. At present only native applications can post to Twitter, and even then only when you explicitly use them to send to the service.

Over time we may see further third-party applications post using the settings stored in the OS.

[4] To send a message to a contact on Twitter, open the Contacts application and find their card. If they have signed up to Twitter then their username should appear in the dedicated Twitter box. Tap this, followed by Tweet to send them a message.

[5] Your message is sent as a mention so will also be visible to anyone else who follows both you and them. To make it private, replace the leading @ with a D followed by a space. You can optionally add your location, which is drawn from the iPhone's GPS chip, by tapping Add Location. Keep an eye on the message length countdown, bottom right.

Tweeting from applications

Several of the native iOS applications let you send tweets directly from their share menus. There work in much the same way as the Share Sheets that Apple introduced to OS X with Mountain Lion.

The range of choices open to you when it comes to sharing data will be tailored on a per-app basis, with some offering more options than others, but in general Twitter is well supported.

Many sport an action button, which looks like an arrow coming out of a box, which opens up your sharing options, but others, such as maps (see right) have a dedicated sharing button stowed away on a secondary page.

Tweeting from Maps

Twitter is a great way to organise a meeting with your friends. If you want to do so on an ad-hoc basis then you can use the iOS Maps application to tweek suggested locations to your friends.

Start by locating your chosen spot on the map by using the regular search tools. Maps will drop a marker on the map identifying the destination, on the end of which you'll see an arrow in a blue circle.

Tap the arrow to switch to the information pane (see below) and then tap Share Location. You'll see the regular choice of sharing methods, so tap Twitter and the location will be tagged to a new Twitter message.

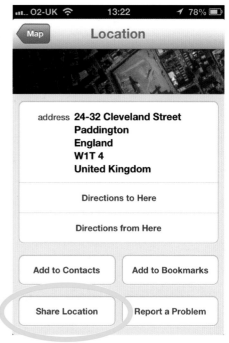

Tweeting from Safari

Twitter is a great way to share links with family and friends, and a well populated Twitter stream with links relevant to a single subject can often attract a strong following from others who have an interest in that field. To tweet directly from Safari visit the page that you want to publicise and then tap the shortcut button on the toolbar. This picks up the regular menu for adding bookmarks or saving a link to the file to your reading list, which in iOS 5 now also includes an option to Tweet. All you need do is write a short covering note to explain to your followers what the linked page is about and your iPhone will send it straight to your followers.

Tweeting from a different account

iOS allows you to sign in to more than one Twitter account at a time and switch between them depending on what you want to post. This lets you separate your subjects according to the interests of your followers with, say, gardening tweets going to one group and your general thoughts and opinions to another.

To change between the two accounts, follow whichever method is relevant to the content you want to post, and when the tweeting interface is displayed tap on the username of whichever account is currently active. This will call up a tumbler showing all of the accounts you have entered, allowing you to choose.

Facebook

Facebook has finally joined Twitter as the second social network in iOS. Signing in through the iOS Settings App works in much the same way as signing in to Twitter, and it allows you to share content with your Facebook friends directly from both native and third-party iOS applications.

Once again, just like when you sign up with Twitter, it offers to update your contacts by adding their Facebook account details and photos to your Contacts book. Those that have been added will have a Facebook 'f' stamped on their avatars (see below).

Enabling your Facebook account on iOS also allows it to add your Facebook events to your calendar and keep them updated, and activates the post to Facebook button on the sharing shortcut in various iOS applications. Over time, as you add new applications from the App Store, they will also be able to use your Facebook login details if you specifically grant them access. Only do this if you understand what rights they will have to post to your wall and access your friends' data and contact information.

Posting to Facebook from iOS 6

[1] The easiest way to send a quick update to Facebook without opening a Facebook client is to pull down on the clock to open Notification Center and then tap in the Tap to Post box.

[2] However, you can also post content direct from other applications installed on your iPhone. Here we are using the Photos application and have tapped the share button on the lower toolbar. This calls up the various ways in which you can share your content with friends, at the centre of which is the Facebook option. Tap this.

[3] This calls up the Facebook posting card with the photo that we want to post to our account clipped to it. Here we are writing a short description so that it makes sense when it appears on our account, as it's not immediately obvious what the image depicts. We can geo-locate it by tapping the Add Location link below it and tap Post to send it.

[4] Facebook lets you organise your contacts into groups, and you can make your post visible to just a small selection by tapping Friends in the lower right corner of the card and selecting a group.

iBooks

Apple is hoping that the iPhone will become a book replacement. It's not the first company to have this idea, as the likes of Sony (with the Reader) and Amazon (with the Kindle) already have competing products.

Of course, iBooks in itself probably isn't enough to entice anyone to buy an iPhone. Apple's interest, then, most likely lies more in selling content, and to that end it has developed its own iBooks Store, which works along very similar lines to the App Store and iTunes Store and can also be accessed on the iPad.

How to buy a book

1. Open iBooks and tap the Store button on the toolbar at the top of the application. The app flips around to reveal the Store hiding behind it as though it was a secret doorway.

2. Browse the store. Use the different options on the toolbar at the foot of the app to check out the charts, browse categories or search for a book by author name, title or keyword. The index is extensive, and it's easy to find almost any book you're after. Bear in mind, though, that not every book published in print is available in iBooks. Likewise, not every book available digitally is also available in print. When you've found the book you want, click SAMPLE to download the first couple of chapters for free.

3. The sample is delivered to your shelves, with a 'SAMPLE' strap slashed across one corner so you know at a glance that it's not the complete volume. Tap it to read the contents. Samples are generally fairly generous, so you can get a good idea of the writing style and thrust of the story.

4. When you get to the end of the sample, you're given the button to download the complete volume, at which point you'll be charged. If you don't want the rest of the book, you can keep the sample for free.

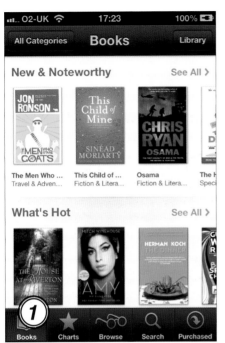

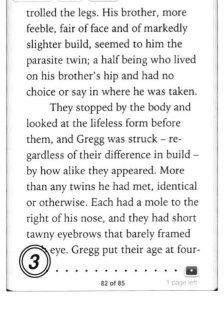

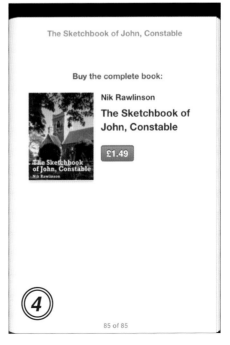

Your books are arranged on shelves, a little like the albums in the iPod application. Tapping one opens it on the screen, in your choice of font and text size. This is managed through the font setting dialogue that hides behind the AA button at the top of each page (see right). Tap this and choose between smaller and larger characters in seven common fonts. The sider above this controls the brightness of the display so that you can tailor it to your own particular eyes and the lighting conditions around you, while Themes lets you set the colours used.

To the right of both of this is a picture of a magnifying glass, which signifies the search tool (opposite page). Tap this and enter your search term and it will hunt through the book you're reading to find every instance of that word combination. If it remains ambiguous, Search Web and Search Wikipedia buttons at the bottom of the results panel let you search online for more information.

Each time you open a book, iBooks will remember where you left it last time, so you shouldn't ever lose your place, and if you're on the contents page of a book you'll see a resume button at the top of the page that, when tapped, takes you to your last-opened page. However, you can also set bookmarks throughout the text by simply tapping the bookmark logo in the top right corner of any page (if you can't see this, briefly tap the main body of the screen to call up the iBooks toolbar. You can set several bookmarks in this way and they will all be organised on the Bookmarks page of the book's index screen.

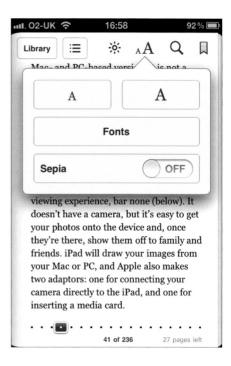

The longer you use iBooks, the more you'll fall in love with this way of reading, with a progress bar at the bottom of the screen showing how far through the book you have read, and the integrated dictionary ensuring you are never lost in a sea of unfamiliar words.

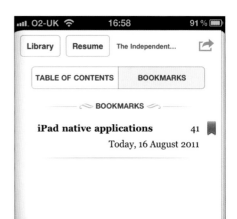

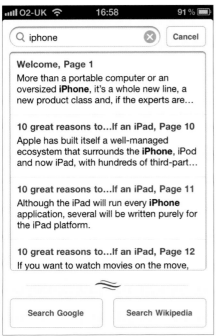

Above: iBooks' integrated search tool will find reference to pages in your current book, and extend the search to Google and Wikipedia should you choose.

Above left: Don't spend your time squinting. iBook gives you a choice of seven fonts in a wide range of sizes.

Above right: You can't use a pencil to make notes in your digital books' margins, but you can highlight on-screen text and type your thoughts and memos. These are synchronised across all of your iOS devices on which the book is installed.

Left: Bookmarks are stored alongside the table of contents.

Taking notes

iBooks is a great learning tool, allowing you to carry a whole library of books wherever you go and use spare moments to revise. To help you keep note of important sections, iBooks has an in-built highlighting tool.

To use it, hold your finger on the screen to select one of the words from your selection, then release it. Drag the spots at either end of the selection to enlarge it so that it encompasses the whole of the section you want to include, and then select Highlight from the pop-up menu that appears above the selection.

Hightlights are stored in the app's Bookmarks section.

Maps

The Maps application has had an complete overhaul in iOS 6. Previously the iPhone's native navigation tool had drawn down its cartographic data from Google Maps, but as Apple moves away from using Google services (the YouTube app has also disappeared in this latest release of the operating system) it has switched it out for its own online mapping system.

For the end user this shouldn't make too big a difference. You can still switch between different map types, including a regular plan view and satellite imagery, you can check on the traffic and plan a route by car, foot or public transport. Just about the only thing missing is Google Street View.

It still ties in with other iPhone applications, too, providing third-party mapping and location services to third-party add-ons, and helping you plot your contacts' details from the Contacts application or addresses in their emails..

Browsing

Unless you've moved it into a folder, Maps is found on the iPhone Home screen, and each time you launch it, it will pick up from wherever you last left off. The best way to get to know it is to simply browse around. Drag your finger across the screen to pull the map in any direction. After taking a moment to stream the next section from the Internet it will update, to show you the settlements, roads

and named businesses in the newly-uncovered area.

Try zooming in by placing two fingers on the screen and slowly drawing them apart, then do the same in reverse, pinching them together to zoom out.

But street plans are only half of the story. As the Maps application takes its data from a centralised server, it also has access to high resolution aerial

Tap the curled up icon on the Maps toolbar to call up the application options, which include a choice of three maps and a list of travel directions.

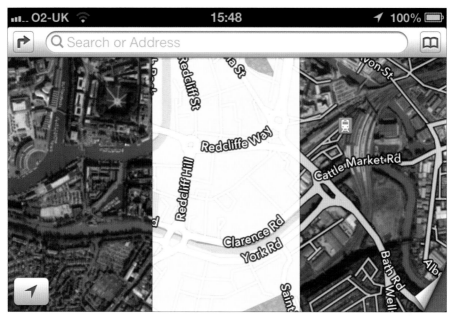

Three parts of the same map. These panes each show the same area of Bristol rendered using the satellite, standard and hybrid views respectively.

photography for much of the world, and this can also be streamed to the iPhone, then scrolled, zoomed and searched in exactly the same way. To switch between the two, tap the button in the lower right corner of the interface with the curling paper icon to call up the underlying menu, which lets you pick between standard, hybrid or satellite.

Hybrid overlays the standard plan-style map over the downloaded aerial photography so you can see not only the buildings and geographic features on the ground but also labels showing where they are. The hybrid view is particularly clever, as not only does it allow you to re-size the photography while keeping the maps proportionally accurate, but it will also intelligently tailor the amount of

information shown on the maps to avoid blotting out the photography.

So, when you are at city level rather than building level it will show only the major arteries instead of every single road, and change the size of the font used to label them so that it remains legible. This way you can use a wide area overview to get yourself to more or less the right location before zooming to a more appropriate scale when you need to start navigating individual roads.

iOS 6 introduces proper 3D views to the satellite maps. Available on the iPhone 4S and 5, and the iPad 2, this feature is called Flyover, and it renders the centres of important cities fully so you can see how the buildings relate to one another. Twisting your fingers on the screen lets you turn them around. Dragging, meanwhile, lets you fly across them.

Searching

You can't spend your whole life dragging a map around. It would be like taping together every Ordnance Survey sheet and then carefully folding and re-folding them every time you wanted to look at a different part of the country. It's far better to jump straight to the map you want, in

both the paper- and pixel-based worlds, which is where searching comes in.

Tap inside the input box and enter a search query. This can be very specific or quite general; it understands landmarks as well as addresses. For example, White House, Washington DC, will take you straight there for a view that is best seen using satellite imagery rather than the plain old map. Likewise, 30 Cleveland Street, London, UK, will accurately pinpoint the home of Dennis Publishing, at which point we would recommend switching back to the map view.

But what if you are out and about and you desperately need a local service?

Flyover lets you explore cities as though you were seeing them from a helicopter.

Searching for what you want is enough to call up associated businesses.

That is when searching with business names comes to the fore. You are in Seattle, the home of coffee, and need a caffeine hit to start the day. Tap in the search box and type coffee, and a volley of pins will drop onto the map, each marking out an outlet.

Tapping each one brings up its name on an attached tag, on the end of which you will see a small arrow in a circle. Tap an arrow and the map will slide off the screen to reveal that outlet's contact details, giving you the address, phone number, email details, website and other supplementary information.

Where am I?

An easier way to see exactly where you are, which is particularly handy if you are in the middle of a large city, is to use the self-positioning tool. Tap the compass pointer icon in the bottom-left corner of the screen and the map will re-centre and be overlaid with a blue circle. Your position will be within that ring.

The iPhone 3G and later primarily use GPS to get a fix on your position, if possible. GPS works by receiving a stream of data from a constellation of satellites orbiting the earth. These satellites transmit a time code and their current position. The iPhone looks at the time codes and compares their accuracy. By working out how much they differ, it can work out how long it took the time codes to reach it from each satellite, and thus how far away the receivers are. When it has a fix on two or more satellites (the more the better) it can then draw a

virtual line from each one, and where they converge will always be its position.

If the iPhone can't get a perfect fix on the satellites, perhaps because of cloud cover, trees overhead or the fact that it is inside a building, it augments this information with supplementary information received from the cellphone network, various public wifi networks and your own personal wifi network. Together these provide supplementary triangulation information that enable it to estimate your current location. This same supplementary technology works on the original iPhone, which lacks the GPS-receiving hardware.

You are here: tap the compass arrow and your current location is picked out in blue.

Route planning

Searching is only half of the story, though. It's no good finding a coffee shop you want to visit if you don't then know how to get there. Fortunately the Maps app has a set of very accomplished route planning tools that can help in this respect, giving you street-by-street and turn-by-turn directions to a great degree of accuracy for towns and cities all over the world.

1. Either tap the location finder if you want to navigate from your current position, or search for a location in the regular way.Tap on the market that shows the result, followed by the blue arrow to see the contact details sheet. You'll see two options on the page that follows: Directions To Here and Directions From Here. Pick the latter.

2. This location will be automatically entered into one half of the directions equation. All you need do now is enter your destiation into the other half of the pair. Do this and then tap Return.

3. Maps draws up a selection of routes for your journey. You can tap between them to see how they differ, but you should always find that Route 1 is the shortest in terms of time taken, if not actual miles travelled.

4. Pick the route you want to use and then tap the start button. Immediately your iPhone zooms in to the first step of the journey so that you can see more clearly what you need to do. When you have

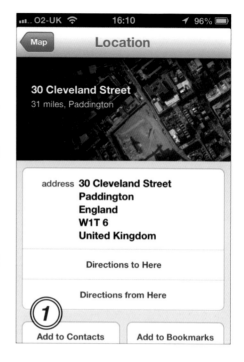

completed the first instruction, swipe it to the left to move to the next one. Continue doing this as you work your way through the journey. You might want to travel with a companion who can do this for you so that you can keep your eyes on the road.

5. If you would find it easier to follow a list of written directions that you can scroll, rather than stepping point by point through a map, then tap the Overview button at the top of the screen, followed by the button with three lines on it at the bottom. This opens a list of written directions with turn signs on each line.

You can now drag the list up and down to see what is coming up around the corner. If you want to see how the layout of the road relates to each step, choose the one you want to examine and tap on it to switch back to the map view.

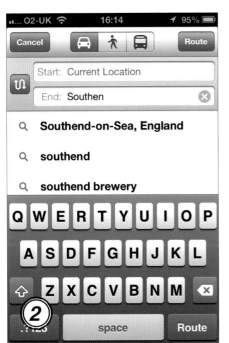

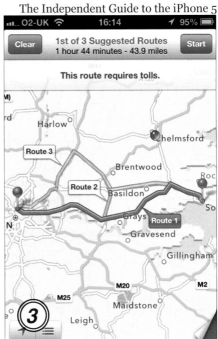

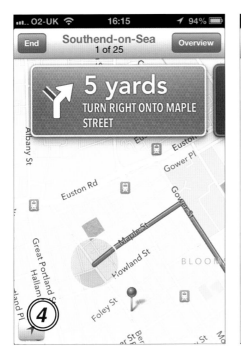

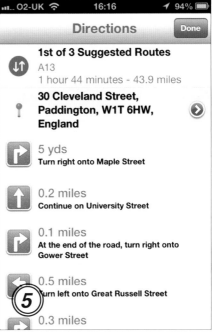

Mapping the traffic

Maps also knows about the traffic conditions on major roads through some of the UK's and other countries' largest connurbations. It is activated from the same options menu as you use to switch between the satellite, map and hybrid views.

This feature colours up the roads in the current window according to how well (or poorly) the traffic is flowing along them. Roads without any markings on them are a good choice for the busy traveller as they are flowing freely. Those that have a red dashed line following their route, though, are congested, and so you may want to steer clear of them.

Taking a hike

The Maps app isn't just there to help stranded drivers find their way around; you can also use it to plan a route that you intend to take by foot.

Start out by planning your journey in the same way as you would for a car journey but use the buttons at the top of the list of results to switch from private transport to walking. Logically, you tap the picture of the walking man to do this.

Naturally when you switch from car to foot you can take some tracks that wouldn't be suitable for a car but you should also expect the journey time to be increased by a considerable amount. Be warned.

NEW IN iOS 6

Setting your language

It's all very well having accurate directions to help you navigate, but if you're in a foreign country it might be more confusing than helpful if the street signs and directions don't match. In this instance, switch to the Maps settings (in the Settings application) and set Always English to OFF. That way the maps will display place names for which there are also English variants in the local language (see grabs below).

While you're there, select the most appropriate 'Distances' setting to match the local screen signs so that you always know when your turn off is approaching on busy roads.

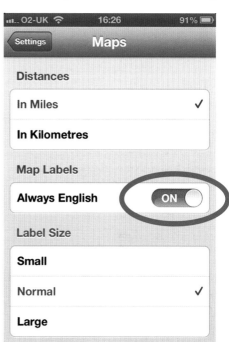

iCloud

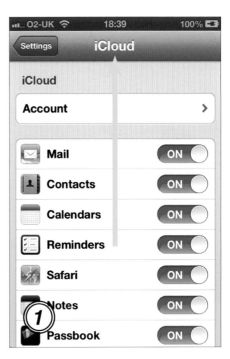

iCloud is Apple's online backup and synchronisation service. It also has tools for managing your email, organising your contacts and maintaining your calendar.

It launched in autumn 2011 as a replacement for the company's long-running MobileMe service.

Signing up for an iCloud account is free and can be done directly from an iPhone running iOS 5 or iOS 6.

[a] Open Settings | Mail, Contacts, Calendar | Add Account and tap the iCloud icon at the top of the list.

[b] You need an Apple ID to sign up for iCloud, so tap Get a Free Apple ID and enter the details that Apple needs to set up your account. When complete you can use your Apple ID to log in to iCloud.

Managing your iCloud storage

Each iCloud account comes with 5GB of free storage. You can pay to increase this, but it makes sense to monitor your usage to avoid this if you can.

[1] Tap Settings | iCloud and scroll the page past the various settings. Tap Storage & Backup.

[2] The Storage & Backup page shows you how much space you're using. We've used less than 1MB. Tap Manage Storage to see what is using your capacity.

[3] One of our apps, Pages, is using 8.6MB of storage on our account. As Pages is stored locally on our iPhone we know that this is purely consumed by docs. Tap Pages to see which ones.

[4] The largest file in our iCloud account is a 480KB document. That's not a great deal of space, but as we're not using it any more we may as well remove it anyway. Tap the toolbar Edit button and then use the bar icons to the left of each file to bring up their dedicated Delete buttons. Tap Delete to remove the file.

[5] If you can't delete any of your files but still need more room to work with, return to the Storage & Backup page and tap Change Storage Plan. Apple gives you the choice of either 20GB or 50GB of additional space. You choose.

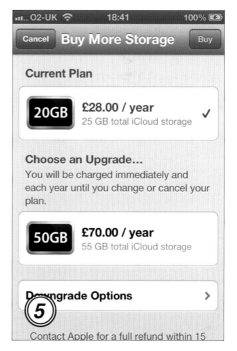

Photo Stream

iCloud can store up to 1000 of your most recent images in what it calls a Photo Stream. These images can be taken on any iOS device and, because they're stored on Apple's servers, they're available to all other iOS devices logged in to your iCloud account. This way, the photo you took on you iPhone could be inserted into a Keynote slide that you're designing on your iPad.

Images are also stored on your Mac, if you have one, in the iPhoto application, and on a PC in a specified folder so now you can shoot as many pictures as you like and they'll turn up on your computer.

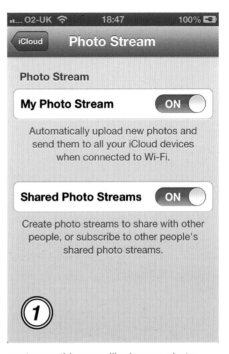

[1] Make sure the iCloud Photo Stream is enabled by tapping Settings > iCloud > Photo Stream and tapping the ON/OFF slider so that it shows ON.

[2] Open the Pictures application, where you will see a Photo Stream button on the toolbar. Tap this and, if you have taken any photos on another iOS 5- or iOS 6-enabled device logged into an iCloud account with Photo Stream active they will automatically appear here. Images you taken on your local iPhone obviously won't be sent here as they are stored in the Camera Roll, but they will appear in this album on other iOS 5 devices. The space taken up by the images in your Photo Stream doesn't count against the 5GB free iCloud allowance.

[3] Images are automatically expired from your photo stream after 30 days, so if you

spot something you like in your photo stream over that time that was taken using an alternative iOS device then you'll need to make sure you manually save it to your local photo store if you want to keep it. Tap the Edit button on the toolbar, then tap on each of the images you want to save. They will be greyed out and have a tick overlaid on them. If you tap one by mistake, tap it again to deselect it. When you have finished, tap Save and select a folder to which you want to save them.

[4] The next time you fire up iPhoto on your Mac while connected to the Internet it will download the contents of your Photo Stream and use it to update its own internal library. Unlike your live Photo Stream, iPhoto doesn't retire images from the library so there's no need to manually copy them if you want to keep a copy.

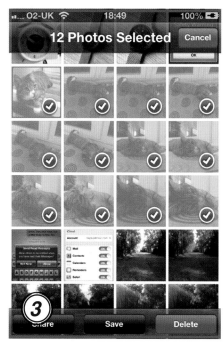

Sharing a Photo Stream

When it launched, Photo Stream was designed purely for personal use, but in iOS 6 you can also share your Photo Streams with other users.

Again, you'll need to select the images you want to work with, as you did when saving images to your Camera Roll, by tapping Edit and then tapping each one in turn. *[5]* After that, tap the shortcut button and select Photo Stream. Enter the address of the contact with whom you want to share it, give the stream a name and choose whether it should be available to the public, then tap Next and,

optionally, add a comment before making it live by tapping Post. *[6]*

When your contact receives the invitation email it will contain a direct link to your shared Photo Stream, which is just as well, as the link is extremely long and would be impossible to remember, not to mention difficult to type in directly.

If you later want to revoke a public or shared Photo Stream, tap Photos | Photo Stream *[7]*, then tap the arrow on the right of the name of the Photo Stream you want to get rid of *[8]*, followed by Delete Photo Stream at the bottom of the panel. *[9]*

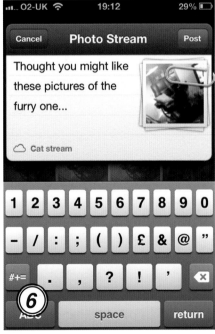

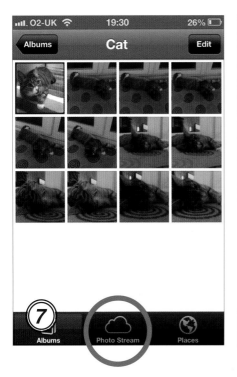

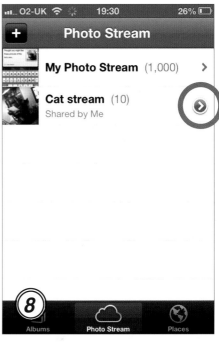

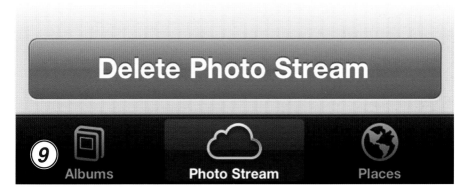

APP OF THE WEEK

GAM

GAMES

955 Dreams

Band Of The Day

☆☆☆☆☆ 23 Ratings

Alamofire

Gowalla

ERES MY
ATER?

OF THE WEEK

STREETMUSEU
LONDINI

APP OF THE V

ape-and-share
ames

iTunes
festival
London
2011

COLDP

Stream the Free S
for a Limited Ti

Apps

Section 3

FREE >

motai

THE

The App Store

For many people, the biggest problem with the original iPhone was that it was a closed, sealed unit. And we're not just talking about the hardware, for just as you couldn't change or upgrade the battery, you also couldn't install your own applications. Well, not legally, anyway.

In truth some enterprising owners found workarounds that allowed them to hack a way into the iPhone's system and add their own applications to its core system files – or those they had downloaded from the net. It worked, but it was risky, as Apple didn't authorise such modifications. This meant that some users who had hacked their iPhone discovered that it no longer worked after downloading a firmware update.

Known as Jailbreaking, this practice continues, with many users now Jailbreaking their old, out-of-warranty devices that can no longer receive updates to iOS, or more recent devices on which they want to install applications that haven't been authorised for sale through the App Store.

Apps go official

Recognising that app development was a fertile market from which it could profit, Apple soon announced a Software Development Kit, and a store through

The iPhone's in-built App Store lets you buy and install applications directly.

which developers could sell their work. It's not surprising, then, that by the time he stepped on stage to announce the iPhone 3G, around a half of Steve Jobs' script concerned itself with the new applications that had been written specifically for the iPhone by third-party developers and Apple itself.

Every application on the App Store, which is accessed through iTunes on your Mac or PC, or the App Store application

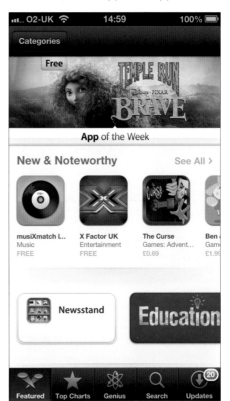

on your iPhone, must be approved by Apple. This sounds draconian, but it's not surprising: few network operators are happy to have their users installing their own software onto their handsets for fear that they may cause damage to the networks themselves.

They can be free or charged for, and all are developed using Apple's free Software Development Kit. Before they can have their applications certified for

use on the iPhone, however, developers must pay a $99 registration fee that buys them an electronic certificate to prove to Apple who they are, and that they are a reliable developer.

Large applications must be downloaded through iTunes on your Mac or PC or by Wifi, but applications of 10MB or less, can be downloaded wirelessly over the mobile phone network direct to the handset itself. Each one is registered on the phone, which monitors the App Store for updates and notifies you of any that are updated editions available for download by posting a small red number beside the App Store icon.

For developers, Jobs outlined six key benefits in developing for the iPhone and distributing applications through the App Store. Key among these was the fact that the developer gets to keep 70% of revenues, and that they themselves can pick the price at which they sell their products – so long as they match specific price-points set by Apple. Apart from the wide range of free applications on the Store, the cheapest software costs just 69p (in the UK) or 99c (in the US and Europe) to download.

Other benefits include access to Apple's payment mechanism, meaning that developers don't have to deal with credit card payments themselves (which

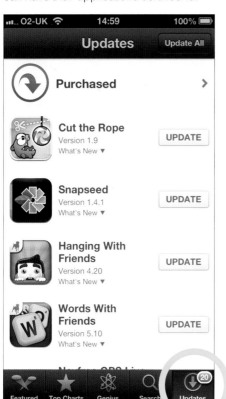

It's easy to see when you have updates available, courtesy of the counter badge.

is also a benefit for us end-users as it means we are always dealing with a trusted company – Apple), no hosting costs, no marketing fees and, perhaps most important of all, regular payments.

More impressive, from a developer's point of view, is that as the applications are hosted within the iTunes Store, they benefit from Apple's own digital rights management software, FairPlay, so end-users won't be able to buy a single copy and then pass them around between one another.

If you would like to try your own hand at developing applications for the iPhone, the software development kit can be downloaded from *developer.apple.com/programs/ios* (see grab, below).

App Store applications

So what can you expect to find on the App Store? The complete catalogue runs the full gamut, all the way from games to business applications. Key among the games that were demonstrated during the original App Store launch was Super Monkey Ball, which uses the integrated accelerometer to roll a moving ball as you tilt the iPhone forwards and backwards, and side to side, through 110 levels of play. An eBay application lets you

track and bid on auctions without using the web browser, and the team behind WordPress has ported an edition of its hosted blogging software to run on the iPhone, allowing you to update readers on your latest train delay while you are still sitting in the carriage. Perhaps most excitingly, this latter application will even let you post pictures from the iPhone's camera straight to your blog. If you wanted to post iPhone photos to an online journal before, you first had to download them to your computer.

Fans of social networking will welcome the many tools for uploading images direct to Flickr, chatting with friends on Twitter and updating your Facebook status and posting to friends' Walls. You might wonder why you'd want either of these two latter applications when iOS 6 has both Twitter and Facebook built in, but in truth they're key to gaining a fully-features experience on either social network without resorting to the browser.

If you would rather not rely on trawling the web yourself or using an online RSS reader application then check out one of the main RSS reader applications, or indeed the dedicated newspaper applications from some of the UK's biggest broadsheet and tabloid publishers. For your fortnightly fix of Mac

In many cases it can be easier to search for and buy applications within the App Store inside iTunes, from which they can be synchronised with your iPhone, iPad or iPod.

and iPhone news, be sure to search for MacUser's application, which presents a digital copy of every issue for viewing on an iPhone or iPad screen.

All can be reviewed and rated so you can see what others thought of each one before you spend any money, but do bear in mind that most often those who give ratings to anything from a holiday to a service to an app are those who have not enjoyed the experience rather than those who have. How often do we feel more motivated to complain rather than complement, after all? Far less than when we've had a bad experience, in almost every instance. It's therefore worth reading a few reviews rather than stopping after the first bad one.

Use the search tools to find applications on the basis of name or function, or use the Genius function to have the App Store make recommendations formulated by examining your previous purchases.

Signing up for downloads

Before you can download anything from an Apple Store, of which the App Store is a part, just like the iTunes Store, you need to sign up for an Apple ID. If you have downloaded music from the Store for use on an iPod then you already have an ID – just as you have if you are an iCloud or former MobileMe or .Mac subscriber. If not, then the easiest way to get yourself an Apple ID is within the iPhone itself. Tap Settings > Mail, Contacts, Calendars > Add Account... > iCloud > Get Free Apple ID.

Synchronised downloads

Since the introduction of iCloud, Apple has enabled App synchronisation on iOS. Switching this on through Settings > iTunes & App Stores, where you can apply separate options for music, apps and books, means that any compatible application downloaded on your Mac, PC, iPad or iPod touch will be simultaneously downloaded to your iPhone, and vice-versa (see below).

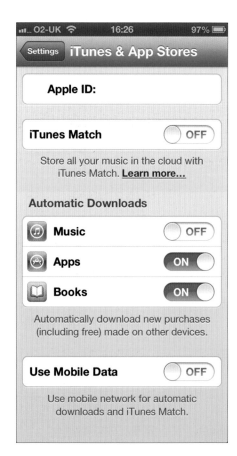

Buying applications on iOS

Although you can download applications using iTunes on your Mac or PC, it's even easier to download through your iPhone.

Apple maintains extensive lists of the best-selling paid-for apps and most popular free applications, but the smartest way to find what you're looking for is to search directly.

Start the App Store application and tap the Search button on the toolbar at the bottom of the screen, then use the search box at the top of the screen to enter a keyword, subject, app name or publisher. Here we have searched for Dennis Publishing (see above left), which has turned up an extensive list of magazine

applications published by the publisher of this MagBook.

The results of your search are presented in a sideways-scrolling set of panels. Swipe through them until you find the one you're after – in this case, PC Pro – and then either tap the button to directly install it or, if it's already installed on your iPhone, open it. If it's a charged-for application, the price will be displayed below the application name.

If you're unsure whether or not you've found the app you're after, tap the application icon at the top of the panel to open further details, including screen grabs (see above right), reviews from other users and a list of related applications that might also interest you.

Pages
Keynote
Numbers

iWork for iPhone

Pages, Keynote and Numbers were the iPad's original killer apps. They haven't left the App Store top 100 since their launch, and now that they're also available on the iPhone the continued popularity of all three apps is all but assured.

Each of the apps gives you the option to create a new document from scratch or copy one from iTunes or a WebDAV server. This latter option is particularly attractive as it allows you to host all of your work on your own server, rather than resorting to a third-party provider.

It also means that should you choose you can host your documents online without using iCloud's syncing services, although in many cases you may have to pay to do this, where iCloud will offer you up to 5GB of storage for free, so you'd need a very good reason to take this option, at least in the first instance.

iCloud entirely revolutionises iWork, on the Mac, iPad and iPhone, making the iPhone just one part of a far larger productivity ecosystem. Previously it was a little impractical to start working on a large document on your phone, knowing that you would have to transfer it later, but that stumbling point has now been fixed, without the use of cables or email.

File handling

Any work you initiate on your iPhone, then, should be waiting on your Mac when you next wake it up, and files created at work should appear on your iPhone for further work on the journey home.

The apps' document managers have been revamped; they're now more flexible than the formerly iPad-only incarnations. Previously documents were displayed in a single row that extended beyond either side of the screen, so that as you scrolled through them only one could be displayed at a time. This made it impractical to

The various iWork apps now support folders in the same manner as iOS.

conventions. Hold down on a document until they all start to shake and the toolbar will change, introducing a trash can for deleting files and a duplicate icon for making copies.

This is an excellent, simple version control tool – particularly if you file your older versions in yet another folder – as it means you can create a new version of any file when you want to take it in a different direction but keep track of what you have created so far.

It's no longer possible to email your documents from the manager. Instead you must open the file you want to send and tap the Tools menu (spanner icon), followed by Share and Print. From here you can email your document, send it to iTunes or copy back it to your WebDAV server in various native and third-party formats. There is no option for creating documents from scratch on WebDAV storage, unfortunately, and due to the lack of a single config file shared by all three apps you have to enter your WebDAV settings once within each app.

The old iWork.com service that Apple ran at a domain of the same name and which allowed iWork users to share their documents online has been retired. This is not entirely surprising as it was a little underwhelming, allowing colleagues to download copies and comment on documents, but not to work on their contents directly in the way that a fully-fledged online office suite like Google Docs or Microsoft Office 365 would do.

keep more than a handful of documents on your device at any one time. Now, however, both the iPhone and iPad versions can display a maximum of nine documents at a time in grid formation, sorted by name or date. Better yet, they can also be organised into folders in the same way as the icons for iOS apps on the home screen: drag one document over another and they're grouped in a new folder. This opens as a split in the interface, as it does for app icons, and can be renamed as appropriate.

This inevitably means that some file management tools have moved. For starters the controls that appeared below each document have disappeared in favour of following further iOS

Each of the iWork applications has print features built in, but to use them out of the box you'll need an AirPrint-compatible printer. These are few and far between at present, but you can tunnel through to any local or remote printer that is already accessible to your Mac by using AirPrint Activator (compatible with OS X 10.5 Leopard and later, free from *bit.ly/lGPGa6*). This is a smart, lightweight workaround that greatly enhances the appeal of the iPhone apps, and runs as a background service on your Mac or PC, so it won't consume space on the Dock of Taskbar once you've set it up.

Apple has made good use of the iPhone accelerometer in implementing a neat shake to undo feature in each of the apps, but it only takes you back one step. Shaking for a second time invokes redo and so replaces the parts of the document that you might just have removed. Neither function is executed without confirmation, fortunately, so you won't undo a commute's worth of typing when your train goes over rough points and shakes you in your seat.

Handling images

Each app also has access to the iOS media browser for inserting images and videos into your documents, but if you don't have iPhoto on your Mac – which will cost you an additional fee to download from the Mac App Store – you'll have to stick with photos taken on your iPhone or saved to your Camera Roll, or the library of shapes that ships as part of each application.

Even then Apple's policy vis-a-vis any movies you might want to use in Keynote is confusing. If you only want to view movies currently on your Mac in the iOS Videos app they can be synchronised directly from your iTunes library, but if you want to use them in iWork you'll have to turn to iPhoto again, first copying them into your library and then returning to iTunes to handle the synchronisation. It's a clumsy work-around that could leave you with two copies of the video on your iPhone in two different locations, potentially consuming twice the capacity in the process and leaving you wondering whether this is an iPhoto sales tool.

Windows users can synchronise photos that they want to use in their iWork documents from their PC to their iPhone by installing the iCloud Control Panel, which is a free download from *apple.com/ icloud/setup/pc.html*

Once installed this resides in the regular Windows Control Panel and lets you specify a local folder into which you would drop any photos you want to use on your iPhone. Dropping images into that folder would automatically synchronise them to your device over iCloud.

At the same time, you would specify another local folder that would be used to accept images sent to your machine from iCloud Photo Stream. It can't be the same one or you would set up a continuous, never-ending loop that would be sending images backwards and forwards between your PC and iCloud non-stop.

You can save a lot of work by recycling assets created in one app within another. Write your text in Pages, for instance, and you can copy and paste it onto a Keynote slide. Likewise, Pages and Keynote will both happily incorporate any graphs you've created in Numbers, and you can even edit the underlying data if you triple-tap the graph image, at which point it spins around to reveal a table with familiar Numbers-style layout and keyboard. Sadly, by this point the data has already become unlinked from the original source, so any changes made in a second application won't be reflected in your Numbers original.

File compatibility

The various iWork applications create rich, beautifully-formatted documents. To store all of the data involved in putting them together it has had to develop its own native file formats. That's not a problem for Mac users, as it also produces a native OS X version of each application, but it's not such good news for Windows users as there's no equivalent available for the PC.

Fortunately, though, each of the applications allows you to share you work in a widely-accepted compatible format by converting your files to Word, Excel or PowerPoint documents. You can also output them as PDF files, which are perfect for publishing online and ensuring not only that your work looks exactly the same on any other device, but also that it's more difficult for someone else to tamper with it and change the contents.

Each of the iWork applications lets you email your data in an Office format.

To convert your work, tap the spanner icon in any of the iWork applications and pick Share and Print > Email, then choose the format you want to use.

System requirements

The various iWork applications are compatible with iPhone 3GS and later, iPod touch (3rd and 4th generation) and iPad. They require iOS 4.2.8 or later.

Although each app works well with the iPhone keyboard, they are greatly enhanced through the use of a Bluetooth keyboard, allowing for more comfortable input of longer tracts of text. They can output material to a printer or connected display using Apple's Dock adaptor.

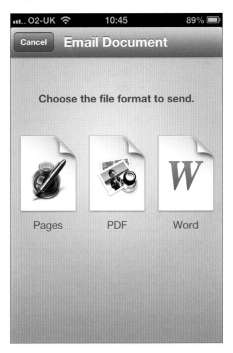

Keynote

Pros Makes it easy to lay out impressive slides + Good transitions engine
Cons No widescreen option
Verdict A wider choice of slide aspect ratios would be welcome, but beyond that Keynote barely puts a foot wrong

Keynote for iPhone is a landscape-only app. This is hardly surprising when you consider the results are likely to be projected or shown on a screen.

There are four default zoom stops – minimum, fit, full screen and maximum. The latter presents your slide at full size, exceeding the screen borders; the first two are surrounded by interface elements, such as the slide channel, toolbar and clock; the third gives over the whole screen to your slide without zooming it beyond the screen dimensions. You switch between them by pinching or unpinching very quickly and immediately removing your fingers from the screen, but for more control a slow movement that keeps your fingers in place lets you move to any zoom point in between.

Keynote ships with a choice of 12 themes, including plain white or black backgrounds. Each contains several page layouts onto which you can drop your own content. Preset frames can be resized or deleted altogether, and each theme includes a blank page if you'd rather start from scratch.

Every theme includes several constituent pages, each of which can be selected and then tailored to your own ends.

Like the OS X version, it has dynamic centre and edge guides to show you when various elements are aligned on the page, with a bubble of coordinates following any object as you drag it around the page. Zoom to full screen or larger and you'll also benefit from pop-up rulers that appear as you drag and disappear when you stop.

Triple-tapping an image lets you zoom it within its bounding box, while holding on it lets you copy, replace or delete. All of these actions come naturally for anyone who is accustomed to using iOS, and as with Pages and Numbers we were impressed by the way in which Apple has broken down complex formatting tasks into simple steps. Animation is a case in point. This is hived away on the Tools menu, but select it and you can tap on the

Above: Keynote has straightened up the intentionally rotated text in this PowerPoint file and padded its previously widescreen slides, neither of which we wanted.

Below: It's easy to give your slides some extra visual impact using the built-in transition animations, which can be applied to complete slides or the elements they contain.

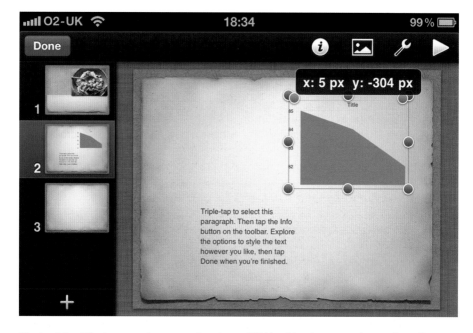

Each of the iWork apps gives you visual feedback when dragging elements. Nowhere is this more important than when building slides in Keynote.

various assets on each slide – or on the slide itself in the organiser channel – and pick from one of 16 different transitions, change the speed at which it executes, the direction of motion and the build order. Many of these are the same as the animations found in the OS X edition, which is impressive considering the different chip architecture. It also includes Magic Move for animating elements that appear on two consecutive slide.

Its shortcomings are few and far between. Chief among them, though, is the inability to specify your own slide size, which is resolutely 4:3 aspect (the

OS X edition lets you choose from five different pixel dimensions, including widescreen dimensions). Some styles, including rotated text, were lost when importing a PowerPoint presentation from our WebDAV server, and although we were impressed that Keynote accepted the file at all we were less impressed that it resized the slides within it by padding them top and bottom to achieve its favoured 4:3 aspect ratio.

Nonetheless, Keynote on the iPhone represents a truly impressive porting of an already first-rate application. It would be possible to build a highly professional presentation from scratch using its sophisticated tools, but for our money its true value lies in being able to present from anywhere and make last minute changes without unpacking a Mac.

Numbers

Pros Extensive 'function' help files
+ Intuitive selections + Data capture
features
Cons None
Verdict The gold standard for mobile
apps, and a truly useful, logical iPhone
port of what was already an impressive
business tool

Numbers is perhaps the most ambitious
iWork app of all, combining calculation,
layout and images which, in the case of
graphs, it generates itself.

You can start a spreadsheet from
scratch or pick one of the 15 pre-defined
templates (16 if you include the blank

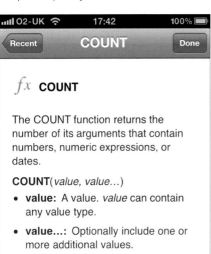

one) that encompass everything from
invoice and expense reports to budgets
and mortgage calculators. Each can be
customised by dragging the on-sheet
elements into new positions. Tables
can have up to five header rows and
columns, which can be frozen to keep
them in view as you pan and scroll. You
can add up to five footer rows, too, at
which point there's little room left on
screen for your data.

Double-tap a cell to edit it, at which
point a keyboard pops up. As with the
iPad edition there are four keyboards to
choose from, depending on the task at
hand. The regular iPhone keyboard is
supplemented by number (digit-centric,
with currency and percentage), time
(months, days, hours and minutes), and
mathematical. The latter option focuses
on numbers and operators, with extensive
help for the uninitiated.

Your most recently-used functions
are organised on a menu of their own,
with the full set of 250 available functions
hived off into a secondary menu and split
into categories. Tap the arrow beside
each one for a full description of its
function and how to use it. You do need
a fair idea of what you're after before you
start looking as there's no way to reverse
look up a function based on what you
want to achieve, but assuming you locate
the one you need it'll be dropped into the
formula bar, leaving you to select the cells
with which it should work.

*Less experienced users will welcome the
extensive help screens that explain how
to use each function.*

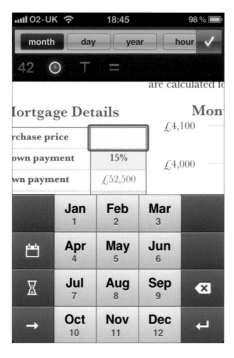

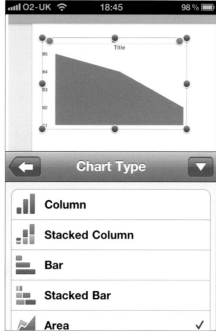

With four keyboards to choose from, Numbers makes data entry quick and easy. Here, the time and date keyboard.

Numbers for iPhone handles graphs with aplomb, creating attractive charts that match those of the OS X version.

The number keyboard is more intelligent than it first appears as it lets you quickly build forms that aggregate their data on a separate sheet, instantly converting the iPhone into a handy data gathering console.

Marking out selections is simple as Numbers seems instinctively to know when you want to drag out a selection area or drag the whole table to pan it. Further, as the formula bar remains active until you explicitly close it by tapping the tick on its furthest end you can select discontiguous cells by dragging

across some and tapping on others as appropriate without a keyboard modifier or any multi-finger gestures (to select multiple objects in Pages, on the other hand, you must hold down on the first while simultaneously tapping subsequent objects with a free finger).

Select a table rather than a cell and smart bars appear above and to its left. Although they're not split in line with your cells they relate specifically to the columns and rows beside them, such that tapping the bar above column B selects the full height of that column and lets you drag it to a new position. Tapping the bar on the left does the same for rows, in one of the most impressive demonstrations we've yet seen of multitouch control.

Numbers is nothing short of a triumph, and although you might not use it for your end-of-year accounts it does let you perform some seriously complex maths on the move, mugging up on finances before a meeting at the bank or capturing regimented data that needn't be reformatted back at base.

The print layout tools are simple but effective, giving you an overview of the finished document's on-page appearance and positioning.

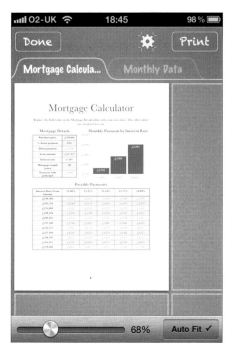

Pages

Pros Well thought-out formatting tools + Enormous font choice
Cons Word compatibility incomplete + Limited page size options
Verdict For anything and everything beyond the abilities of the iOS Notes application, this is the app to go for

Pages ships with 16 templates and although they're not split into the same broad categories as those in the Mac version there's a wide range to choose from. Beside the expected blank document, four letter types and two choices of CV ('resume'), there are more ambitious project proposals, visual reports, posters and fliers. It might seem hopelessly optimistic to set out on creating such complex documents in pretty much any other app, but in Pages Apple's clever thinking has taken away much of the pain. Placeholder text is selected as a single entity when tapped so you can type straight over it, and pre-populated image boxes have picture buttons on them to open your Camera roll with a single tap.

Pages' layout tools are surprisingly accomplished. Leading can be set at quarter-line increments on a scale of 0.5 to 5, text can be flowed into anywhere between one and four columns, and aligned to the left, centre or right, as well as justified. Characters range in size from a fairly unsubtle 9pt to a chunky 288pt and can be set in 58 faces, each with their associated variants – bold, light, italic and so on. Just about the only

Navigate through multi-page documents by dragging through stacked thumbnails.

Pages can work with Word documents, and will warn you of any problems.

limitation is the choice of paper sizes, which runs to just A4 and US Letter.

Perhaps most impressive, though, is the step-by-step process involved in formatting your document. Pages is a portrait-only app, so the interface is too narrow to accommodate an extensive horizontal toolbar. Apple has overcome this by giving over half of the display – the space occupied by the keyboard when you're typing – to formatting panes. Each tap takes you further into the settings, so a tap on the 'i' opens the panel, from where 'Style' opens the formatting pane. Within this pane, 'Text Options' takes you

into the character formatting controls and 'Font' lets you pick a typeface. You're now four steps down, but the whole process is so intuitive that you won't get lost, and there's no need to climb back up through the formatting stack unless you want to make changes elsewhere – tapping your document on the upper half of the screen takes you straight back to what you were working on, applying the changes in the process.

Likewise, each editing operation is treated as a single discrete process. Tap your text to rewrite it and the Documents button on the toolbar, which usually takes you back to the file manager, is swapped for a Done button to be tapped when you've finished. It may sound fragmented, but within your first few minutes of use it seems so natural that you barely notice the inevitable to-ing and fro-ing.

Word compatibility is fair, but not flawless, with some fundamental elements, such as text boxes and shapes stripped out upon import. The question, though, is whether Pages is any more useful than the iOS Notes app. Certainly it's more ambitious and kicks Notes into

a cocked hat for features, but if all you want to do is tap out a few words without waking up your Mac then Notes holds two trump cards: it costs nothing and it has a horizontal keyboard option. What it lacks, though, is Pages' sharing tools. The only way to get your data out of Notes is to email it or connect to iTunes either using the Dock connector or wirelessly over your local network. That, plus Pages' extensive formatting controls, allows us to recommend it with a clear conscience over its competitors.

Pages ships with 16 impressive templates. Customising them is a simple matter of swapping out the placeholder elements simply by tapping.

Despite the limited screen space, Pages' thoughtful UI design fits in a lot of features into the lower portion of the screen without getting cluttered.

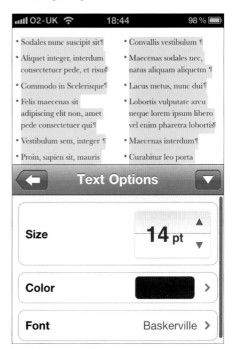

Using iWork with iCloud

By setting up data synchronisation you can use iCloud as a conduit between your Mac and iPhone so that all of the work you create in iWork on one is automatically available to you on the other, so you no longer need to email it back and forth. Here we'll walk you through setting it up for the first time.

[1] The first step is to ensure that you have enabled synchronisation for your iWork applications. Tap Settings | iCloud | Documents & Data and make sure that the ON/OFF slider is set to ON. By default iCloud only synchronises your application data over a wifi network, but if you will be away from wifi for a long time and want to make sure that all of your work is backed up all the time consider tapping the slider beside Use Mobile to also send it over the 3G network.

Although we are concerning ourselved with iWork here, the same Documents & Data synchronisation allows you to work cross-platform with other applications that have used Apple's iCloud interface, such as ByWord and iA Writer on the Mac and iPhone.

[2] Open one of the iPhone iWork applications and you'll see that it synchronses each of your documents with any copies it holds on the server. You can save them onto the server either by copying them manually through the web interface or by creating them in another iCloud-aware installation of iWork on an iOS device.

[3] Now it's time to create a new document. Tap the '+' button on the toolbar at the top of the file management screen, followed by the large Create Document button and choose the template you'd like to use. You won't need to give your document a name right away, so just dive straight in and start typing. All the while you're doing so iWork will be backing up your work to iCloud in the background.

[4] When you have finished working on your document log in to your account at icloud.com and click the application icon in the top left corner. Choose iWork from the menu and then click Pages to see your saved documents. Your new document will appear in the first space.

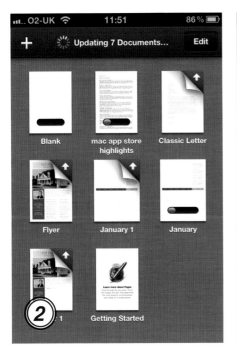

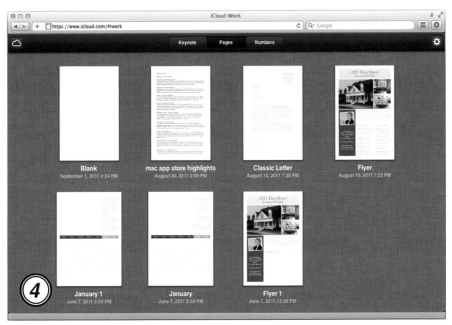

iCloud Document Libraries on OS X

When it shipped Mountain Lion, Apple introduced iCloud Document Libraries. This is a core feature of the operating system that third party developers can plug in to their applications. Once they've done so they can create and save documents on your iCloud account, and you can access them directly through the file save dialog. That means that you can access the stored files on your iPhone.

Apple updated its three OS X-based iWork applications to work with iCloud Document Libraries on the same day that it shipped Mountain Lion. It was a very small update, which apart from catering for the Retina Display on the new MacBook Pro gave them the ability to directly access documents in iCloud.

Apple has made the underlying code that facilitates this feature available to all developers who want to incorporate it into their own applications, which means that third-party tools, like the excellent distraction-free word processor, ByWord, supported iCloud documents already.

Like the iOS edition, the Mac interface for handling iCloud documents allows for simple file management tasks. Dragging the icon for one file on the top of another gathers them both into a single folder that you can go on to rename as appropriate.

Using iCloud Document Libraries

iCloud Document Libraries are effectively a Mac-based view of your online server space. They don't offer a great deal of functionality other than basic organisation and file management tasks, as you'd find in a regular file save dialog. However, they do greatly simplify the task of working with your online files.

iCloud Document Libraries sports the familiar iOS file management tools

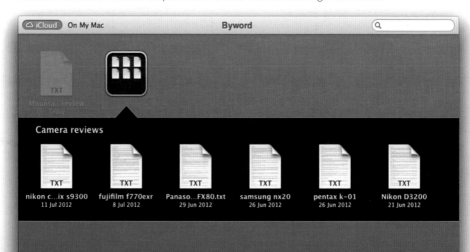

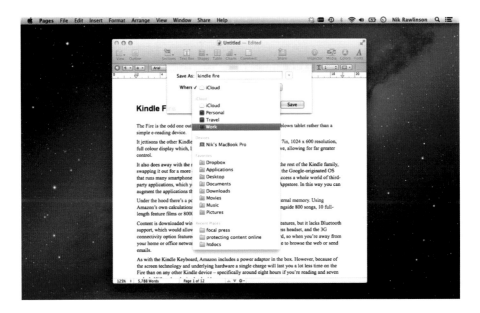

For example, the file open dialogue includes a Mountain Lion Share Sheet, hidden behind the shortcut button, which lets you send your document to another remote user by email or using Messages or, if you're using a wifi-enabled Mac, share it with another wifi Mac on the same network through AirDrop.

When it comes to saving your files back out of your application and onto the server, the folders you have set up in your iCloud storage space are presented as sub-folders inside a new iCloud category in the destinations and devices drop-down. This makes it far easier to use iCloud as a destination than any alternative third-party server technology, and should do much to encourage greater adoption of iCloud which, as is becoming apparent, should be a key selling point of the Apple ecosystem.

Above: Mac OS X applications that make use of iCloud Document Libraries, such as Pages, allow you to save files directly to folders stored in iCloud.

Below: You can also email files straight out of iCloud when using Mountain Lion. This saves you using the export function in the iOS iWork applications.

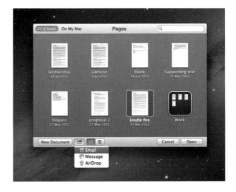

iPhoto

iPhoto has long been one of the best photo management apps on the Mac, and now it's available on iOS, too. It's not installed by default, but rather is a paid-for download from the App Store.

On iOS it's naturally been somewhat slimmed down – especially where the iPhone is concerned – but you can still use it to organise your photos into collections, edit them and upload them to the net to share with friends and family.

Here we'll walk you through the most common editing and publishing tasks so that wherever you happen to be you won't have to wait until you get back home to start being creative with your photos.

iPhoto interface

iPhoto files your photos on a series of virtual shelves (below). You will notice that the albums on the shelves match the albums in the Photos application. To keep them in sync, iPhoto will frequently update your library, which will require that you pause what you're doing for a short time.

The toolbar at the bottom of the screen is where you navigate the different parts of the application, with Albums

and Photos being fairly self-explanatory options. The Events entry will only make sense to anyone who uses iPhoto on their Mac, and mirrors the Event into which photos are organised in that application on the Mac. You can decide which of your Mac-based Events are shared with your iPhone when syncing it through iTunes.

The penultimate option is Journals, which are an iPhoto-exclusive feature through which you can gather together your best photos and publish them online in a digital photo album.

The cog at the end of the row opens iPhoto options. It's worth taking a look at this, and if you're running out of battery power consider switching off the Wireless Beaming feature as this relies on Bluetooth, which will consumer power.

Working with photos

To start working with your photos, either tap Photos on the toolbar and select a shot, or open an album from the Albums screen and pick one from there. The layout of the screen that follows is determined by the orientation of your phone, with portrait phones showing a strip of thumbnails for the shots in your album along the bottom of the screen, and a landscape phone showing them in a sidebar column.

Tap the photo you want to work with and it will be displayed in the larger part of the window, with a range of

management tools stripped above it. See below for a run-down of each of those tools and what they do.

The most useful among them at this point are button 4, which lets you view information about how the image was shot and add your own notes, and button 3, which lets you share it using the regular iPhone controls, including emailing, posting it to Twitter and sending it to your Flickr account. This is also where you'd turn if you wanted to beam the photo over Bluetooth to another iOS device running iPhoto.

Button 5 – the curled up photo – flips back and forwards between your original shot and an edited version of the same. When you first open an image it doesn't do anything as you won't have made any changes to it. That's what we'll cover off next, so select the image you want to work with, and then tap Edit.

iPhoto image management controls

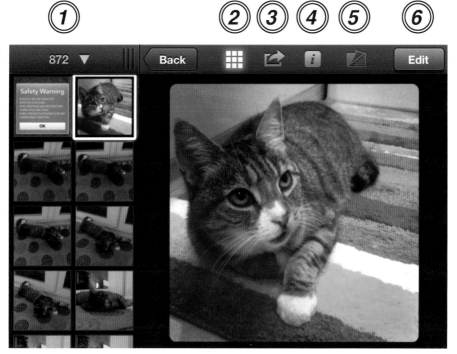

[1] Tap to open menu and select a range of photos; *[2]* Show / hide thumbnails sidebar or footer; *[3]* Share, print, email or publish the current photo; *[4]* View or edit photo info; *[5]* Swap between original and edited image; *[6]* Open full photo editing tools.

Editing photos

When you enter the editing mode, turn your attention to the new toolbar that appears at the bottom of the screen. This contains all of iPhoto's creative controls.

The main toolbar, explained below, contains only one real editing tool, which lets you apply an automated enhancement to the active photo (right), as determined by iPhoto itself. Often this will be enough to improve your image all that it needs, but if you want to take things further then simply tap button 1 – the toolbox – to open the full editing tools.

The tools have been designed to be extremely easy to use. They require no real knowledge of image manupulation and are all managed through simple taps, pinches and twists on the controls.

The first toolbar, shown to the right, lets you crop your images by dragging their edges in towards the centre, or open up secondary toolbars using other buttons.

Exposure presents you with a simple toolbar that allows you to change the balance between light and dark, or tweak the contrast and brightness. You can make similar changes directly by tapping

on the photo. Adjust the highlights, for example, by tapping and dragging left and right or up and down on the brightest part of the image, and do the same with the darkest part to work on the shadows.

The Colour control lets you change the tone of your image, again by dragging sliders or parts of the image directly (see the four-way arrow in the grab on the opposite page).

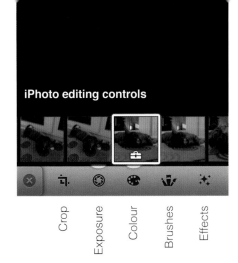

iPhoto editing controls

Crop Exposure Colour Brushes Effects

iPhoto image manupulation controls

[1] Open full editing controls; *[2]* Auto enhance; *[3]* Rotate image by 90 degrees (tap to turn it further); *[4]* Flag for follow up; *[5]* Set as a favourite; *[6]* Hide this photo; *[7]* Open settings and options; *[8]* The toolbox icon indicates that image has been edited.

Each of these changes is applied across the whole image, so you should be careful with precisely how your edits are being applied. Specifically you should try and make sure that the people in your images don't have unrealistic skin tones as this will be immediately obvious. The easiest way to do this is to instruct iPhoto to preserve skin tones itself by opening the tool options by clicking the cog icon at the end of the toolbar and tapping the slider beside Preserve Skin Tones so that it is set to ON (see above, right).

Selective editing

However, you can also apply some images selectively to only specific parts

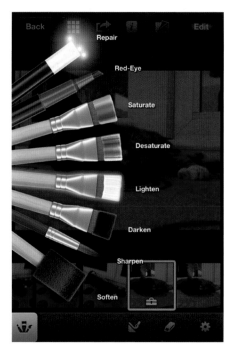

of the image by using the brushes. Again, these are called up from the toolbar.

There are eight brushes in the toolbox, each of which performs a different function (see grab, below left). With careful use of the Lighten or Darken brushes you can apply exposure changes to specific parts of your image; likewise, you can apply more controlled adjustments to the colours in your image using the Saturate and Desaturate brushes.

To work with these brushes, select one and then paint on the parts of your image to which you want to apply the result.

It's difficult to see which parts of the image you have painted over when using any of these brushes in their default state, so tap the cog icon to open their settings panes and make sure that the sider beside Show Strokes is set to ON. The brush will then lay down red strokes to show you where it has been applied so that you can make sure you have covered every part of the image that you need to edit (see grab, opposite page).

This is particularly helpful in allowing you to see when you might have painted your adjustment on some parts of the image that you need to leave untouched.

In this instance, return to the settings screen and tap Erase Saturate Strokes, or to start again tap Erase All.

Sharing your work

When you have finished editing your photos, tapping Edit takes you back to the image management screens, ready to be shared with friends and family.

The easiest way to share them is obviously to email, Tweet or post them to Facebook, but iPhoto also allows you to create more impressive Journals, each of which can contain up to 200 images.

Start by tapping the share shortcut on the management toolbar, followed by

Journal. Tap Choose... and then select each of the images you want to include in the Journal by tapping on them one at a time. Each one will be ticked to show that it's been selected.

When you have finished, tap Next and give your new Journal a name, then scroll through the six different album designs until you find one that you like.

This is the last step, so tap Create Journal, followed by Show to preview it. If it looks the way you intended you can use it as a slideshow, sent it to iTunes or share it online. If you want to share it online, tap the Share shortcut button again and select iCloud as the destination, followed by the ON/OFF slider.

Turning on strokes when using the brushes makes it easy to see which parts of the image you will affect when you apply your changes as they are highlighted in red.

GarageBand

GarageBand is Apple's easy to use music creation application. Although you can record real instruments and vocals with it, you don't actually need to have any musical talent to put together a competent composition, as you can drag and drop Apple's pre-produced musical loops into the composition in any order you choose to build up a song without setting your hands on a single real-world instrument.

Over the next four pages we'll show you how you can create your first composition using GarageBand. So, fire up the app and get your fingers tapping. You're in for some musical fun...

We're going to create our song using Apple's pre-defined loops, but we still need to select an instrument to get started. This will create the first track in our song. We've selected the Smart Keyboard (see grab, above). When you're

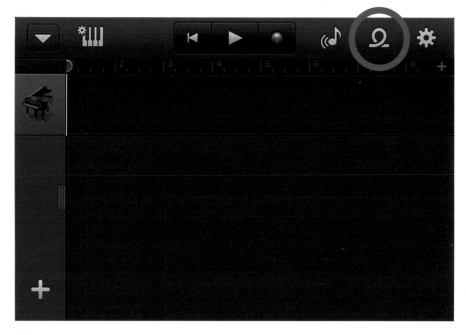

comfortable with the interface, switch to the tracks layout by tapping the button with horizontal lines on it in the upper left corner of the GarageBand interface.

This opens the track view where all of the instruments we have recorded using GarageBand will send their output (see grab, opposite page, bottom). For those with little or no musical talent it's also the place to turn if you want to drag and drop pre-recorded loops onto the stave to build up a track using Apple's bundled material. Tap the loops button, which we've circled, then select Synths.

You can audition each loop for every instrument in the library by tapping it in the lower portion of the Loops dialogue (see grab, above). Tap through them until you find one that you like the sound of. The bars measurement to the right of each name tells you how long each one lasts. To use a loop, simply drag it into the workspace. It's automatically given its own track in the recording, indicated by a thumbnail of the associated instrument. We're going to start with Euro Party Slicer FX, which runs for four bars. This obviously isn't going to be long enough for a whole song, so we'll adjust its length.

You can lengthen and and shorten a loop by dragging on the ends of the sample, and needn't increase it so that it repeats in neat blocks of the full length of the sample if you only want to repeat a small portion. GarageBand loops have all been recorded in such a way that when you extend them the repeated opening portion runs off perfectly from the last few notes, so you can repeat them infinitely.

We've set our sample to loop itself so that it fills up the existing track. We now need to add the other parts of our song by dragging them out from the loop selector. We don't want to add any further synth tracks; instead we want to work with another instrument. Tapping Instrument takes us back to the instrument selector.

We've opened the drum loops. There are plenty to choose from, and as yet we haven't dragged one into our composition. That's because we need to filter the selection until it contains only those examples that would work well with those other parts of our composition already in place. Therefore, we've tapped the loops dialogue's Descriptors line, and will now tap Processed to see only those effects that have been worked on (see grab, following page).

Applying a descriptor significantly reduced the number of drums that met our requirements, making it easy to find one that worked well with the synth track that was already in place. Having auditioned each of the results we settled on Hip Hop Berlin Beat 01 and dragged it into the workspace. We want this to cut in after the first cycle of the synth loop, so we've positioned it so that its opening beat, which you can see indicated by the peaks and troughs in the soundwave, lines up with the first note after the second break in the synth track. We've played it back a few times to make sure the two are in sync (see grab, below).

With a synth, drums and now two vocal tracks, our song is starting to sound like a finished production. However, with so much else going on our vocal tracks

are starting to get drowned out by the music that surrounds them. We'll fix this by reducing the volume of the synth. By default the volume controls are hidden, so slide out the sidebar to its full width by holding on the grab-handle on its right-hand edge and swiping into the workspace to reveal the controls. Drag the volume slider until the synth volume is more appropriate to accommodate the other parts of the track. You can mute it entirely by tapping the speaker.

The one thing our track is still missing is a compelling beat that will tie together all of the other parts of the composition. Although we have dropped in a pre-recorded drum loop at parts we want to highlight, we also want to record our own additional drum track that will run throughout the whole of the song. Tap '+' to add a new track, then switch back to the instruments and scroll through until you get to Drums. Tap it to select.

GarageBand now presents you with a complete drum kit. You can switch between different kit styles – each with an appropriate matching sound of its own – by tapping the Classic Studio Kit button at the top of the screen.

We're happy with this selection, so after a little rehearsal we're ready to add our self-drummed track to the song. Having made sure that the progress marker is at the start of the track, we tap the toolbar record button and start playing our drums in time to the pre-recorded part of our composition, which will play in the background. The composition will loop around, while a metronome keeps time in the background.

Switching back to the track organiser we can see that our drum track is now in place on a track of its own, with dotted highlights showing where our beats fall. This allows us to drag it around as we did with the other tracks so that each beat lines up with a significant part of our pre-recorded loops. We can also change the volume, as we did with the synthesiser.

All we need to do now is apply a little processing to our composition to give it a professional finish. We'll do this by passing selected tracks through the Audio Recorder. Select the track you want to process and double-tap its icon in the sidebar. We can now play back the track and apply a selection of effects by tapping them on the right of the screen, before saving and sharing.

Cases

There are plenty of iPhone cases to choose from, but Uunique's selection for iPhone 5 are among the smartest we've seen. The range is leather-backed throughout, with a choice of conventional red, black and grey clip-on hard-cases, embossed leathers immitating crocodile, ostrich and snake skin. Each hard case is priced at £25, and they're extremely slimline, so won't turn your sleek new iPhone 5 into a clumpy lump. The folio case, far left, is a more traditional fold-over soft leather cover, which holds the iPhone extremely snugly, protecting both the back of the case and, when closed, the screen. A small magnet keeps the cover closed, and the interior surface is again leather, with a soft brushed finish. It costs £30.

www.uunique.uk.com

Glossary

3G Third-generation mobile phone network technology offering speeds high enough to enable rudimentary video conferencing and mobile television streaming. It is widely available across much of Europe, but was first introduced for public consumption in Japan in 2001.

802.11A/b/g/n Wireless communications standards. See wifi.

AAC Advanced Audio Coding. Audio file format favoured by Apple due to its high quality and ability to incorporate digital rights management features. It is the default format for tracks downloaded from iTunes Store, or ripped from CD.

Bitrate Means of expressing the number of audio samples processed in a set period of time, usually a second. See also kilobits per second.

Bluetooth Short-range radio networking standard, allowing compatible devices to 'see' and interrogate each other to discover their shared abilities and then use these abilities to swap information. It is commonly used to connect mobile phones and headsets for hands-free calling, but is also seen on keyboards and mice used with desktop computers.

Dock Cradle designed for use with an iPhone or iPod that supports the device while it is charging and transfers data to and from a host computer using a bundled 30-pin connector.

Digital Rights Management DRM. Additional encoded data added to a digitised piece of audio or video that controls the way in which it will work, usually preventing it from being shared among several users. See also FairPlay.

Edge Exchange Data rates for GSM Evolution is the network technology used in the first iPhone upon its introduction in the US and Europe. It offers higher speeds than 2.5G networks, but lower speeds than the battery-hungry 3G.

Encoding The process of capturing an analogue data source, such as a sound or an image, and translating it into a digital format. Although files can be encoded with no loss of quality, the process usually also involves compression to reduce the resulting file sizes.

FairPlay Digital rights management system developed and used by Apple. It is a closed, proprietary system that Apple has so far refused to license to third-party software and hardware manufacturers, or to music owners on the basis that this could lead to its compromise.

Home Screen As used within this book, the term used to describe the screen within the iPhone's interface that displays the icons for the installed applications

iCloud Online synchronisation service owned and run by Apple from several data centres around the world. Provides backup services for iPhones, iPads, iPod touches and other Apple hardware, and shares both documents and images. See also iTunes Match.

IMAP Internet Message Access Protocol. A server-based means of hosting incoming and outgoing email messages such that they can be accessed using a remote client such as the iPhone. The primary benefit of working in this way is that the messages will always be accessible from any device, anywhere and at any time.

iOS Short for iPhone Operating System. The underlying software that enables your iPhone to start up and run third-party applications. Currently on its fifth revision – iOS 5 – it is based on the same code as OS X and was previously called iPhone OS, despite its use on the iPod touch.

iPad Portable computer device invented and sold by Apple. It uses the same operating system as the iPhone and can run compatible applications, but boasts a 9.7in screen, making it easier to type on than the iPhone or iPod touch. Does not have phone features, but connects to the Internet by means of wifi or a 3G cellphone network connection.

iTunes Music management software produced by Apple, also used to manage the connection between an iPhone and Mac or PC. It gives access to the iTunes Store for purchasing music, audiobooks and video content, and will also handle podcast subscriptions.

iTunes Match Online music service that lets you stream your music collection from the Internet.

Kilobits per second (Kbps) A measurement of the number of audio samples that go to make each second of music in a digitally encoded track. The higher this number, the smoother the sound wave will be, and the truer to the original it will sound.

Megapixel One million pixels. A measurement used to quantify the ability of a digital camera to capture information. The higher the megapixel measurement, the more information it will capture, leading to larger file sizes, but allowing for the captured image to be either printed on a larger scale or cropped to highlight smaller details. It is a common misconception that higher megapixel counts lead to sharper images, which is not always the case, as image crispness often depends as much on the quality of the lens in front of the sensor and the relative size of the sensor, rather than resolution, of the sensor itself.

MP3 Shorthand term used to denote audio tracks encoded using the Motion Picture Expert Group codec 2 (Mpeg-2), level three. Arguably the most common audio format found on the web thanks to its widespread use by portable music players. Capable of being read by the iPhone and iPod, but it is not Apple's preferred format.

OS X Operating system developed by Apple, a variant of which is used inside the iPhone and later versions of the iPod under the name iOS. It shares a common core with Apple's modern operating system for laptop and desktop computers, Mac OS X, which was developed from code it inherited when it acquired Steve Jobs' NeXT computer company. The X in its name is pronounced 'ten' since it is the tenth major iteration of the operating system.

PAC Porting Authorisation Code. This is the alphanumeric code you need to obtain from your existing mobile phone network operator to move your number (port it) to a different network so that you can use it on a new phone or take your handset with you, even if you have run past the end of your contract. This will be required if you want to transfer an existing mobile phone number to an iPhone.

Playlist Menu of audio tracks or video files waiting to be played. The iPhone, iPad and iPod are all able to share playlists with those created on a computer using iTunes.

Podcast Pre-recorded audio or video programme distributed over the Internet and optimised for playback on portable devices such as the iPod and iPhone.

Push email The technology by which emails are sent from the central server that holds them to a client device, such as a mobile phone or BlackBerry, without the owner having to manually instigate a retrieval for their messages. This is implemented on the iPhone through Apple's own subscription-based MobileMe or iCloud service.

SIM Subscriber Identity Module. The small half-stamp-sized (or smaller) card found in every digital phone handset that identifies it on the network, containing its number and other data.

SMS Short Message Service. Commonly referred to as text messages, SMS is a means of sending brief notes between mobile handsets, which was initially developed as a means for network operators to send messages to their subscribers. SMS messages are generally restricted to 160 characters or fewer, although many phones – including the iPhone – can thread together multiple discrete messages to make a single, longer communication.

SSL Secure Sockets Layer. A method used to encrypt data sent across wireless connections and the Internet so that it is less easy for uninvited third parties to intercept and decode .

Sync Short for synchronise. The means of swapping data between the iPhone and a desktop or laptop computer so that the information on each – including music, photos, contacts and so on – mirrors the other. Traditionally performed by connecting the two using the bundled Dock connector cable, although Apple is now enabling wireless synchronisation on a local wifi network for those devices running iOS 5 or later connecting to iTunes 10.5 or later.

Toolbar Any area within a piece of software that houses buttons to perform common functions. On the iPhone, most system-based toolbars, such as those found in Safari, run along the bottom of the screen, while navigation buttons generally appear at the top. This is an unwritten rule, however, and many applications – both from Apple and third-party developers – are increasingly putting controls at the top of the application Window. Pages, for example, clusters many of its formatting tools on a strip at the top of the screen.

VBR Variable Bit Rate. A means of varying the effective audio resolution of a sound file, such as a song, based on the complexity of its contents. More complex sections of a track will thus have a higher bitrate, while less complex parts will be more heavily compressed.